What If Nobody Forgave?

What if Nobody Forgave?

and Other Stories

Edited by Colleen M. McDonald

SKINNER HOUSE BOOKS

BOSTON

First Edition copyright © 1999 by the Unitarian Universalist Association.
Second Edition copyright © 2003 by the Unitarian Universalist
Association. All rights reserved.

Published by Skinner House Books.
Skinner House Books is an imprint of the
Unitarian Universalist Association,
a liberal religious organization with more
than 1,000 congregations in the U.S. and Canada.
25 Beacon Street, Boston, MA 02108-2800.

Cover design and text design by Kathryn Sky-Peck.

Printed in Canada

ISBN 1-55896-442-8

06 05 04 03 02
10 9 8 7 6 5 4 3 2 1

Library of Congress Cataloging-in-Publication Data

What if nobody forgave and other stories / edited by
    Colleen M. McDonald.--2nd ed.
        p. cm.
    Rev. ed. of: What if nobody forgave and other stories of principle.
    Includes bibliographical references.
    ISBN 1-55896-442-8 (alk. paper)
        1. Unitarian Universalists--Education. 2. Religious education of
    children. 3. Storytelling in Christian education. I. McDonald, Colleen.
    II. What if nobody forgave and other stories of principle.
    BX9819 .W48 2003
    268'.89132--dc21   2002030209

Contents

We Accept One Another and Keep on Learning Together

The Day the Turkey Walked

A Candle for Us

Everyone Must Be Free to Search for What Is True and Right in Life

Grandmother's Gift

A Little Jar Labeled Freedom

Answer Mountain

Grady Asks Why

We Should Care for Our Earth and Its Plants and Animals

Preface

From Buddha to Jesus to the Sufi masters, spiritual teachers have used stories to convey basic messages about truth and right living. The tales gathered here are based on themes that reflect the principles of Unitarian Universalism, a pluralistic religion that draws on the values and wisdom of all world religions. These principles affirm that

- each and every person is important,
- all people should be treated fairly,
- we accept one another and keep on learning together,
- everyone must be free to search for what is true and right in life,
- it is our responsibility to work for a peaceful, fair, and free world,
- all people should have a voice and a vote about things that concern them,
- we should care for our earth and its plants and animals.

These collected pieces were chosen for their potential to engage both children and adults in shared worship or educational experiences. Follow-up questions for discussion and a variety of activities designed to appeal to a range of learning styles have been included to enhance the usefulness of the stories as teaching aids. A short list of other tales on similar themes is offered to extend and enrich the experience of reading or hearing each story.

In these pages you will find a resource for family story time, home schooling, religious education and camp programming, and class use. It is our hope that these stories will challenge, inform, and inspire children of all ages.

Telling Stories

The stories in this book were created to be presented in front of an audience. In this context, telling the story is usually more effective than simply reading it aloud.

Storytelling is a skill that can be developed and improved with practice. It is helpful to have a fairly good memory and imagination, as well as an affinity for the spotlight, but a storyteller's main asset is an enthusiasm about the stories and a passion for sharing them with others.

There are various strategies that enhance storytelling. Notes at the end of several of the stories recommend specific techniques, including puppetry, audience participation, and the incorporation of music.

Here are some general tips on how to be a good storyteller:

■ Develop your skills with "natural" storytelling experiences in which you relate your own experience. Choose a memorable and/or dramatic moment from the everyday—the first time you met your spouse, the day you became a parent, an outdoor adventure, a mistake or a triumph—and play it back in your mind as though you are watching a film. Get in touch with sensory details. Recall your feelings. Then tell your story to a partner, vividly and with emotion. Speak in the first person and the present tense, inviting the listener to *experience* the event rather than merely hear about it.

■ When presenting someone else's story, don't be concerned with memorizing every detail and repeating the whole thing perfectly, word for word.

Storytelling encompasses a degree of license, inviting you to make the story your own; tell it from *your* point of view and, if necessary, adapt it for your particular audience. You may want to condense the story to fit into a given time frame, omit or change something insignificant (perhaps a character's name) in order to facilitate memorization, or add your own slant in order to heighten the drama or bring out the message. Of course, you will want to be careful about maintaining the accuracy of any story you offer as factual, and if you make any substantial changes to someone else's story, it is appropriate to communicate to your audience that you have adapted the original.

■ When possible, tell the story in the first person (even if it isn't yours), offering a brief introduction that identifies the character or perspective you are about to represent. This approach conveys an immediacy that makes the story more "real." (Don't be surprised if your audience—forgetting your initial disclaimer—is fooled into thinking the story represents something that really happened to you!)

■ Work at using your voice as effectively as possible. Change it as you speak for different characters. Adjust your tone to go loud and soft.

If a character sings, incorporate a melody rather than simply speaking the words. Tape record yourself telling the story and then listen for energy and variety. You may need to turn up the emotion or ham it up a little in order for your voice to convey your true passion and enthusiasm.

■ Practice, practice, practice. Tell a story to yourself over and over again before sharing it with an audience. Don't memorize by rote—let the story come alive and "happen" to you. Let it become part of your own experience. Then when it's time to go "on stage," relax. Good stories, well rehearsed, almost tell themselves!

—COLLEEN M. McDONALD

Each
and Every
Person Is
Important

If Christmas Eve Happened Today

by Shannon Bernard

We have heard about a birth of a child on Christmas Eve, as the old story is told—something that happened many, many years ago. But what if such a child were born today? The story might go something like this:

Imagine that your parents are quite young, and they don't have much money. Your mom is very pregnant with you, and your folks are excited about having a baby. But they get a notice that they will have to drive all the way into New York City[1] to pay their taxes. The trip will not be easy, with your mom so pregnant, and your family's old car is a bit of a clinker.

It's late afternoon and already dark when they start out. There's some ice on the windshield, and the heater in the car doesn't work well.[2]

Suddenly, as your dad is driving on the expressway,[3] your mom says, "Oh my, the baby is coming!" Your dad looks around. They're not in a great neighborhood but up ahead he sees a star—a Texaco star—and he drives off the expressway, following the light of the star to the gas station.

The owner of the gas station says, "We don't have any place for a baby," but when he sees how scared your parents are, he piles clean rags in a corner and yells for his sister, who is in the back room. Her name is Maria Shepherd.

And you are born.[4]

Maria calls next door for all her children, the little Shepherds.[5] They come in, excited to see a baby. They bring toys they love, and they give them to you as your first presents.

All of a sudden, there is a roar outside. Everybody looks around, and in walk three Hell's Angels on Harleys.[6] They come looking for the service station attendant and instead see your mom and your dad, and you, newly born. One of them takes off his leather jacket to cover you. Another puts a shiny ring of keys down for you to play with. The third looks at your dad's car, shakes his head, and gives your father some money.

The star over the gas station shines. Christmas music can be heard on the radio.[7]

The miracle of the Christmas story is not about angels or even stars. It's not about where or how you were born. The miracle is that you *were* born, that *each* of us was born.

Each night a child is born is a holy night.[8]

NOTE: *This story was written for a live audience and intended to have musical accompaniment; the musical inserts are noted, for those who wish to share this story with a group. The author suggests that a keyboard player or choral group offer a few bars of the specified Christmas carol at the designated spots.*

1. *In telling this story, you may want to name another large city closer to where you live.*

2. *Musical insert:* O Little Town of Bethlehem.

3. *In telling this story, you may want to name a specific expressway closer to where you live.*

4. *Musical insert:* Go Tell It on the Mountain

5. *Musical insert:* The First Noel

6. *Musical insert:* We Three Kings

7. *Musical insert:* Silent Night

8. *Musical insert:* Joy to the World

Some questions for you to think about:

- How would you explain the meaning of "each night a child is born is a holy night"?

- How can you finish these sentences?

  I am glad I was born because . . .

  I am glad [person's name] was born because . . .

  Others are glad I was born because . . .

- What advice would you give the parents in this story (or any parents) about how to be a good mom or dad? What do children need to grow up healthy and happy?

- What makes a person important? What makes a person valuable?

- What are miracles? Name some.

Some things for you to do:

◼ Pretend you are one of the people in the story, and retell the story as it happened to you. If you are sharing this story with a group, imagine you are a television reporter; interview various people who were there (for example, the gas station owner, Maria Shepherd, or one of the Hell's Angels) and ask them about what happened there on Christmas Eve.

◼ Draw or construct a "manger scene" for this story, showing the gas station and the different people. (One suggestion: For the people, draw the figures, cut them out, and glue them onto toilet paper tubes.)

◼ Make a poster collage on the theme "Every night a child is born is a holy night." Write the words on a large piece of paper. Glue on pictures of babies and children from magazines, catalogs, and ads. Find pictures that show children's differences as well as similarities.

◼ Rewrite a Christmas carol, changing the words to tell the story of how you came into your family, or to celebrate the birthday of someone else who is special.

◼ Plan an "unbirthday" celebration, real or imaginary, for someone who is special to you. Think up real or imaginary gifts you could give, refreshments you'd like to serve, and activities you could share. Pick one thing you can actually do with or for your special person and then let her/him know what else you dreamed up, making sure to let her/him know why you think s/he's special.

Give
the Ball
to Peetie

by Gary Smith

My friend Barry coaches a boys' basketball team, the Campbell Cougars. Last weekend the Cougars played the TriCity Tigers at the YMCA. When I asked Barry how the game went, he got this big grin on his face. But then he said, "We lost." "You lost?" I asked. "So why are you so happy about it?" This is what he told me:

TriCity probably has the best team in our league—the best defense, the best shooters, and the best rebounders. We knew the Tigers were going to be quite a challenge for us, but we were up for it. I could see that everyone on my team was improving with every game we played— everyone, that is, except for Peetie.

Now there's a rule in the Y league stating that each boy on the team must play at least one quarter in every game—to give everyone a chance to play. But I hadn't given Peetie a chance to play all season—I'd kept him on the bench. Word had gotten out, though, that this was against the rules and that he ought to play.

Our game against the TriCity Tigers was well under way when I decided I'd better follow the rules and send Peetie in—but not yet. The contest was hard fought. As the third quarter wound down, the Tigers were ahead but my Cougars were running up and down the floor, shooting, rebounding, and blocking as best they could. Finally, I took a deep breath and then I tapped Peetie on the shoulder. He waited at the scorer's table for a break in the action, the horn signaling that he could go in as a sub. But when he got into the game he could barely run. When he tried to run too fast, he fell down. Peetie had a mental disability and serious problems with coordination; soon it was obvious to everyone why I had kept him out.

But the game continued; it was as though the Tigers had five players and my Cougars four. Our team would thunder up and down the floor, and no sooner would Peetie get to one end than the boys would rush past him to the other end; he'd turn around and try to catch up with them, all the time watching the game with a big smile on his face, clapping his hands with the crowd.

And then it happened. Someone passed the ball to Peetie. And at that moment, it was as if time had stopped. Peetie just held the ball, and no one else moved. The referees didn't blow their whistles. The TriCity Tigers, who always had their arms up to block a shot, put their arms down. And Peetie, holding the ball as if he really didn't know he had it, started to move toward the basket. No one else took another step. The crowd was silent.

Peetie walked several steps toward the basket and then realized he was supposed to dribble the ball. He dribbled with two hands because he couldn't dribble with one like you're supposed to. Finally he shot toward the basket; it didn't even hit the backboard.

The moment Peetie let go of the ball, the game continued just as it had before. The two teams fought for the rebound, the Tigers came up with the ball, the two teams thundered back down the length of the floor, and TriCity got another basket. After that, when it was the Cougars' turn to take the ball, someone in the crowd yelled, "Give the ball to Peetie!" And so Peetie got the ball again, and once more everything stopped. Peetie, traveling, double dribbling, holding the ball too long, took a shot. This happened four times and on the fourth try, Peetie made a basket.

The crowd went wild. Peetie went back to the bench, and the gang lifted him up on their shoulders. The final buzzer sounded. Though our team had lost, we all felt like winners. Peetie was the hero of the game.

Some questions for you to think about:

- ▧ Is the rule that everyone should get a chance to play a fair rule? Why or why not?

- ▧ How might Peetie benefit from being on a team like this? What could his teammates gain from having him on the team?

- ▧ What does it mean to lose a game and still be a "winner"?

- ▧ What experience(s) have you had with people who have disabilities? Why do other people sometimes feel uncomfortable around people with a disability?

■ What are some things you can't do as well as many other people you know?

Some things for you to do:

■ Create a cooperative game with a basketball (or some other ball) that someone like Peetie could enjoy with a group.

■ Look through magazines and newspaper ads for pictures of people with disabilities enjoying everyday activities. Write a letter of appreciation to a publisher or business that provides these kinds of pictures.

■ With your class, family, or some other group, make a poster: On a large piece of posterboard or mural paper, write "Each and every person is important." On separate slips of paper, write the name of everyone in the group. Then have all the group members pick a name. Each person is to add that person's name to the poster, including words and/or pictures that show something special about that person.

■ Think about a problem someone in this story had (for example, the coach not wanting to send Peetie into the game). Write a letter to an advice columnist, as though you were that person. Then write the answer.

■ Pretend you are a member of a cheerleading or pep squad. Make up a cheer, with words and motions, to encourage players, whether they are playing poorly or well.

All People

Should Be

Treated

Fairly

The Stone on the Mantel

by Colleen M. McDonald

During the pre–Civil War years, a period dominated by slavery, a teacher named Prudence Crandall, who lived from 1803 to 1890, started a school for girls—white girls. A young black girl named Sara Harris, who grew up in Connecticut during these years, dreamed of becoming a teacher. But in order to become a teacher Sara would have to get a good education—and that meant somehow getting into Prudence Crandall's classroom. In those days, African Americans like Sara rarely had a chance to learn more than a little reading and writing and simple math.

When Sara first asked for permission to attend classes, Prudence turned her down—after all, she was a white teacher and her school was for white girls. Sara kept asking, however, and finally Prudence had to do some hard thinking.

Prudence Crandall followed the Quaker religion. Many Quakers believed that slavery was wrong and that people should treat one another like they were members of the same family. Prudence asked herself whether she had a good reason for refusing to let Sara attend her school. She read newspaper articles about the work of the abolitionists, who were trying to abolish (bring an end to) slavery. She stayed up all night reading the Bible and wrestling with her conscience. Finally, Prudence decided she had been wrong and that Sara Harris, just like any other girl, deserved to come to her school.

One day Prudence and her friend Samuel May were having a discussion. "If you take that girl into your school," Samuel said, "there's going to be trouble—no doubt about it."

"Trouble? What kind of trouble?" Prudence wondered. Still, she was ready to take the risk; she knew that accepting Sara as her pupil was the right thing to do.

Samuel was right: There was trouble. The other students accepted Sara, but their parents were upset; they became angry when they learned that a black girl was being treated as an equal. They warned that if Sara continued as a student, they would remove their daughters from the school.

Prudence was in a bind. She couldn't afford to watch her school fail, but she didn't want to let these angry and frightened people tell her what to do. She decided to stop teaching white girls and re-open the school as a boarding school for black girls.

People threw eggs at the school building the night before it re-opened. And when the new pupils took walks together during the school day, people threw rocks at them as well. One Sunday, Prudence walked the girls to church and was astonished to discover the doors were locked against them.

Town meetings were called to discuss the future of the school. But women weren't allowed to go to the meetings and so Prudence was unable to defend herself and her school. The men of the town voted that a school for black children was against the law and that it was illegal for anyone to help Prudence Crandall in any way. Grocers started refusing to sell her any food, and the doctor wouldn't come when someone was sick.

When garbage was thrown down the school well, the water supply wasn't useable for weeks. The school was set on fire. Stones were thrown through the windows. Townspeople were trying to force Prudence to give up but she refused. She believed the reason they were making trouble was that they were afraid, and she forgave them.

On the stone mantel, Prudence kept one of the larger stones that had been thrown through a window. Looking at that stone made some people angry, but Prudence saw the stone as a sign of hope: one day, people would stop throwing stones like that one and use them instead to build more schools.

Prudence received help from Samuel May and other friends who believed in her work. They gave her supplies and money and found lawyers to speak up for her in court. This assistance kept Prudence and her school going for five years.

Finally, on a winter night, townspeople with clubs broke most of the school's windows. It was too cold not to replace the glass, but Prudence feared that people would come back as soon as the new windows were in and that they would break them, too. By this time she was both tired and afraid. She was afraid of her own feelings—all along she had hated what the townspeople were doing, but now she was beginning to hate the people themselves. Prudence didn't want to become so angry that she had no energy left to change things for the better. She knew she had to move on.

Prudence closed her school and went out west, where she worked for peace and women's rights and continued teaching.

Whenever she got discouraged, being with children kept Prudence going. In her seventies she wrote, "I never had any [children] of my own to love, but I love every human being and I want to do what I can for their good."

Some questions for you to think about:

- How did you feel at the end of the story? Why?
- Prudence believed the people who did not want her to teach black girls were afraid. What do you think they were afraid of?
- In what ways was Prudence Crandall courageous?
- Was Prudence a "successful" teacher? Why or why not?
- What do you think is the lesson of this story?

Some things for you to do:

- Make a mural or poster that says "Beautiful People Come in All Colors." Add drawings or pictures from magazines that include people of different races and cultures.

- Find out more about the Quaker religion. (If you belong to a religious community, identify ways in which Quaker beliefs are similar to those of your own religion.)

- Write an imaginary letter to the editor—or create a speech for Prudence, Sara Harris, or one of Prudence's supporters—arguing why Prudence should be allowed to teach black girls.

- Act out a conversation between Prudence and Sara Harris, perhaps when Prudence announces she is going to close the school and move west.

- Imagine tourists are coming to visit the site where Prudence's school was located. What should they know about her story? Design a "historical marker" to mark the site; decide what it will look like and what it will say.

Brown Shoes

by Colleen M. McDonald

Mrs. Beverly wrote the class schedule on the chalkboard every day.

8:30 Spelling

9:00 Math

9:45 Reports

Sometimes the word *surprise* appeared on the afternoon schedule. All morning the students would wonder what the surprise could be. Free time? A field trip? Food?

One morning the surprise began as soon as the school day started. It was something the students never would have guessed. And it wasn't even written on the schedule.

Mrs. Beverly simply announced, "People who wear brown shoes aren't as smart as other people. They aren't as hardworking or as well behaved. In fact," she went on, "people who don't wear brown shoes are better than people who do."

Colleen looked around at her classmates. Was her teacher playing a game? But Mrs. Beverly's face looked serious.

"People with brown shoes don't deserve to sit at the front of the class," Mrs. Beverly continued. "Anyone with brown shoes who's sitting up front must change seats with a non-brown-shoed person in back."

It wasn't until then that Colleen looked down at her feet. Brown shoes. She was wearing brown shoes, and her seat was in the front row. Stacey, who sat next to Colleen and who was wearing tan sandals, raised her hand.

"Should we move our stuff out of our desks?"

"What did I tell you about Brown Shoes' brains?" said Mrs. Beverly. "Of course, Stacey—how are you going to do your work without your things?"

Colleen was glad she hadn't asked that question.

"Come on, Brown Shoes, we don't have all day," Mrs. Beverly instructed.

Colleen grabbed as much as she could carry in one load, hoping she wouldn't drop anything as she traded seats with Steven, who was wearing grey Nikes.

"Don't forget who you are," said Mrs. Beverly, handing each of the Brown Shoes a nametag that said BROWN SHOES. "And don't lose this—or else!"

The "game" continued during reports. Richard, wearing white sneakers, told the class about basketball. Colleen guessed Richard's report had been copied right out of a book.

"Excellent!" exclaimed Mrs. Beverly as Richard took his seat. "People like you put lots of effort into your work."

Then it was Tony's turn; he was wearing brown oxfords. Tony talked about snakes. Afterwards, Mrs. Beverly remarked, "I guess that's all you can expect from a Brown Shoe."

Next, Mrs. Beverly called on Stacey.

Stacey began speaking but Mrs. Beverly interrupted. "Why do Brown Shoes talk so softly you can hardly hear them?" she asked.

When Stacey spoke louder, Mrs. Beverly remarked, "We're not deaf, you know."

Nick, who was wearing a pair of black boots, was the last one up. His report was much shorter than the others.

"Terrific! Brief and to the point," Mrs. Beverly commented.

Colleen decided to take a chance.

"But you told us the report is supposed to last five minutes," she pointed out. "Nick's was only about three."

"If there's one thing I can't stand about Brown Shoes," Mrs. Beverly replied, "it's when they act like know-it-alls."

Before lunch Mrs. Beverly sent Colleen to the office on an errand. By the time Colleen made it back to her room, the class had left for the cafeteria.

"I figured Brown Shoes would have learned to tell time by now," said Mrs. Beverly.

"It's just a game, isn't it?" thought Colleen, who was finally near tears. "I think Mrs. Beverly still likes me."

At recess Mrs. Beverly told the Brown Shoes they couldn't use the drinking fountain or the playground equipment and that they had to stay off the blacktop. She gave them a catcher's mitt—without a ball—and left them on a muddy corner of the field.

None of the Brown Shoes said anything right away.

Finally, Colleen said, "This isn't fair."

Everyone agreed.

"I'm thirsty," said Stacey. "And I'm tired of this. I'm getting a drink from that fountain."

"But Brown Shoes aren't allowed. You'll get in trouble," warned Tony.

"I don't care," said Stacey. She walked over to the fountain; Colleen and Tony followed her.

"What are you doing, Brown Shoes?" asked Steven, interrupting a softball game.

Stacey didn't say anything; she bent down to take a drink.

Nick pushed her down. "Brown Shoes aren't good enough to drink out of our fountain," he said.

"Leave her alone," said Tony. He pushed Nick back.

■ ■ ■

Back in the classroom after recess, Mrs. Beverly said that the experiment was over—it was time to talk. Colleen was already beginning to understand what the "game" was all about. Her class had been studying the Civil Rights period in U.S. history. Not long ago, many people believed white people were better, and deserved more, than people who were darker-skinned. White children and African American children went to different schools. African Americans had to use separate restrooms and drinking fountains, and when they rode city buses they had to sit in the back.

"How did it feel to be treated badly because of the color of your shoes?" asked Mrs. Beverly.

"I got angry," said Stacey.

"I was scared," said Colleen.

"Is it true that people with brown shoes aren't as smart, hardworking, or well-behaved as people who wear shoes of other colors?" asked Mrs. Beverly.

"NO!" the whole class shouted.

"Does having light skin make you a better person than having dark skin?"

"No. Skin color only affects the way you look," said Tony.

Mrs. Beverly continued. "Then is it fair to treat people badly because of the color of their skin?"

"No!" everyone said again.

"You can't change your skin color the way you can change your shoes," said Stacey. "It's something you're born with."

"I'm sorry I pushed you, Stacey," said Nick. "I don't know what got into me."

On the bus ride home, Stacey said, "I never figured my shoes would bring me bad luck today."

"*Bad* luck?" thought Colleen. She'd never forget what she'd learned as a "Brown Shoe."

Yes, she'd been lucky today. In fact, Colleen realized, she was lucky *every* day.

NOTE: *Colleen McDonald was 11 years old and living in northern Virginia when the Reverend Dr. Martin Luther King, Jr., was shot and killed, in the spring of 1968. The following school year, Colleen's sixth-grade teacher used an unusual method to teach her all-white class about racial discrimination. (It is likely she had heard about the eye color experiment used by another teacher, Jane Elliott, in Iowa.) This story is based on Colleen's unforgettable experience in that class.*

Some questions for you to think about:

- What is discrimination?

- At the end of the story Colleen decides she was lucky to have worn brown shoes that day, and that she is lucky every day. Why do you think she feels that way?

- Why did the fight at the water fountain start? (How might Nick have felt about "Brown Shoes"?)

- Was the game a good way or a bad way to teach the class about discrimination? Why?

- Which groups of people face discrimination today?

Some things for you to do:

- Make up a myth or a play explaining why the people of the world have different skin colors.

- Get some liquid tempera paint in "people colors," or the colors brown, white, and pink. Experiment with mixing the colors until you get a shade that is close to your own skin color. Use the color you have mixed to paint a picture of yourself.

- Imagine waking up one morning and discovering that something about you looks very different (maybe your head is turned around backwards, or you've grown an extra arm). Write a poem, rap, or song about what your day is like.

- Make up a card or a ball game for two or more players that has rules that are unfair. Teach the game to someone else. Find out how s/he feels about playing that kind of game. Figure out how to change the rules to make the game fair.

- Make a collage using magazine pictures or draw a poster with the theme "different and the same." On one side show ways that people are different and on the other show things that people have in common.

Mistakes

by Colleen M. McDonald

Carrie's eyes filled with tears as soon as she saw the homework assignment her teacher returned to her. "What did I do wrong this time?" she thought. Miss Holt's fire-engine-red markings signaled Carrie's mistakes like a siren. Carrie stuffed the paper in her desk without even reading her teacher's comments.

English had always been Carrie's best subject. But then she got Miss Holt for a teacher.

Carrie's mother was a reporter. Her father helped Carrie's class with the school newspaper. Carrie knew she was a good writer too. She remembered the story she'd written in second grade, for the fall open house.

"Perfect!" Mrs. Davidson had announced, handing the paper back to Carrie without a mark on it.

Carrie was the only one in the class who didn't have to copy her story over to correct misspelled words.

All last year, Carrie's classmates had begged her to read her stories aloud. And in August her letter to the editor, complaining about the trash on Beger's Beach, had been published in the local newspaper. But whenever she picked up her pen in Miss Holt's class, she felt like a little kid who didn't even know her ABCs.

"Miss Holt is the worst teacher I've ever had!" Carrie complained to her father that evening.

"Worse than the one who brought liver and onions, instead of treats, to class parties?"

"Oh, Dad, I've never had a teacher who did that!"

"Of course not," said her father, smiling. "And I've always thought your teachers were excellent. But what about this Miss Holt—does she let students get away with too much?"

"Hardly," replied Carrie. "She's great at that look that reminds you she's the one in charge."

"Well, does she know her stuff?"

"She acts like she knows everything." Carrie sighed. "She's always using big words— like when Tony said he wasn't ready to give his report, Miss Holt asked him if he'd been 'procrastinating.' I have to get out my dictionary to understand what she's saying."

"Sounds to me like she's a good teacher," said Carrie's dad.

"But she's always criticizing me," Carrie protested. "Last year Mr. Edwards used to write things like 'excellent!' and 'very creative!' on my papers. But when I get an assignment back from Miss Holt, I find comments like 'watch your commas,' and 'avoid run-on sentences.'"

"What did she think of the story you wrote about the time Grandpa accidentally made a tuna sandwich out of cat food?" asked Dad.

"Not much! She handed it back to me today, covered with red marks. I didn't even read the comments."

"Don't be discouraged," said Carrie's father. "Whatever your teacher may think, I know you're a good writer."

Carrie grinned.

"And don't be too quick to judge Miss Holt," he continued. "When you go back to school tomorrow, take a good look at what she had to say about that paper. Maybe there's something there that will make you feel better."

Carrie took the assignment out of her desk as soon as she got to class the next morning. "Watch your exclamation points," Miss Holt had written on one side of the paper.

"Oh, brother!" thought Carrie.

Carrie saw another comment that started out "Poor" and ended with "mistake," but she couldn't read the rest of her teacher's scribble. At least Miss Holt didn't have perfect handwriting!

Then Carrie noticed something that made her mouth drop open: Carrie had written "banana," and Miss Holt had added a second "n," to make it "bannana."

"B-a-n-a-n-a . . . it was spelled right the first time," Carrie said.

Just to make sure, she looked the word up in the dictionary. There it was: "B-a-n-a-n-a." Miss Holt had made a mistake! Carrie couldn't wait to tell her.

During seat work time, Carrie quietly walked up to Miss Holt's desk.

"Miss Holt, on this paper you gave back to me, you circled this word as a misspelling, but I spelled it right. See—there isn't supposed to be another 'n' in 'banana.'"

Miss Holt looked down at the assignment. Carrie didn't know what she had expected her teacher to do, but she certainly wasn't prepared for what happened next.

Miss Holt smiled.

"I stand corrected," she told Carrie.

"That's it?" Carrie asked. "Don't you want to check the dictionary?"

"I bet you've already done that," said Miss Holt. Carrie nodded. "You know, Carrie, that's not the first mistake I've made in class this year, and it won't be the last. I count on bright students like you to let me know it when I goof."

"Bright? Me? You mean you think I'm smart?"

"Of course!"

"Then why do I get so many marks on my homework papers?"

"You're a good writer, Carrie," said Miss Holt. "I figured you already know that. I'm not here just to pat you on the back. I want to help you keep learning so that you can become an even better writer."

"I never thought of that." Carrie was speechless.

"Okay," Carrie said finally, "but I need to know what this says. I couldn't read your handwriting."

Carrie showed her teacher the scribble.

"It says," Miss Holt explained, "'Poor Grandpa! I won't make the same mistake.'"

It wasn't till she was back in her seat that Carrie noticed a little arrow at the bottom of her paper. She turned the paper over. Miss Holt's ruby red writing glowed: "Thanks for the laugh. This essay is good enough to submit to the Scholastic Story Contest."

Some questions for you to think about:

- Why did Carrie think Miss Holt was a bad teacher? How do you think she felt about her at the end of the story? Why?

- Why did Carrie's father think Miss Holt was a good teacher?

- What do you think are the qualities of a good teacher? A good student?

- Have you ever felt one way about a person and then changed your attitude about him or her after you got to know the person better?

- How do we know it when we're wrong?

- Have you ever caught an adult in a mistake? If so, how did that person respond?

Some things for you to do:

- Think of a teacher who has been very important to you. Write an essay about him or her, or make a card or write him or her a thank-you note (and give it to that special teacher, if you can).

- Create Carrie's story about her grandfather accidentally using cat food to make a tuna sandwich, or make up a story about another funny mistake.

- Choose several words from this story (and perhaps from other stories in this book) that are not easy to spell. Use them in a paragraph or puzzle, and spell some of them wrong. Show the paragraph or puzzle to a friend or family member and challenge him or her to pick out the misspelled words.

- Divide the story into scenes, as though it were a play. Illustrate each one with a drawing, or find three "actors" to play the parts of Carrie, Carrie's father, and Miss Holt, and take photos to represent each scene. Underneath each drawing or photo, write a short summary about what is going on.

- Design a crossword poem: At the top of a piece of paper, write the word *student* (going across). Then, underneath either one of the t's, using another color ink, complete the word *teacher* (going down). Choose another color and add more words to describe the characteristics of a good teacher or student. Write them in using the letters in *student* and *teacher*, as though you were making a crossword puzzle. (For example, you could write in *curious*, using the r at the end of *teacher*.)

We Accept One Another and Keep on Learning Together

The Day the Turkey Walked

by Joshua Searle-White

I'll bet you have heard the Thanksgiving story that gets told every year about this time: there were the Pilgrims, and they had a hard first year, and then after they had lived through the first year and the harvest came in, they had a celebration to show their thanks at having survived. Well, things are a bit different now. Now you don't go out into the field to pick the harvest. Where do you go? The grocery store! You go and get a turkey and maybe some corn, sweet potatoes, pumpkin pie, mashed potatoes, vegetables, Jell-O, and cranberry sauce. Maybe a ham, some beans, and stuff to drink; maybe an apple pie, too, and chocolate chip cookie dough ice cream, and . . . well, anyway, you plan a whole big dinner and you invite people over and you eat and eat and eat until you feel like you are going to be sick!

Well, that's the way it usually is.

But not long ago, a family had a very strange Thanksgiving. This family was the Breckenridge family, with Mom and Dad and Katy and Jimmy and Sarah. On Thanksgiving Day, they cooked and worked and planned, and the kids even helped with the mashing and the peeling and stuff, and they were really looking forward to this big dinner, with the turkey and corn and sweet potatoes and mashed potatoes and ice cream and . . . well, all the things I mentioned. And they got it all ready, and Mom called everyone to the table.

But when they all finally sat down to eat and Dad picked up the knife to carve the turkey, something amazing happened. The turkey sat up!

And it said, "Hey, this is for the birds! Forget it! I'm not doing this!"

And it got up and jumped off the table, and ran out of the room. I'm telling you, this was weird! Then the sweet potatoes did the same thing!

They said, "If the turkey's not staying, we're not staying!" and they rolled across the table (rolla-rolla-rolla-rolla-roll) and onto the floor and out the door.

Then the mashed potatoes did the same thing. (If you think it's weird to have a cooked turkey get up and walk, you should have seen the mashed potatoes!) They kind of s-l-i-d across the table and out the door. And the pies and the peas and the corn and the Jell-O (which went wobble-wobble-wobble-wobble), and the rutabagas and the cranberry sauce (which went boodleoodleoodle), and everything else, for that matter. In the space of a minute or two, all the food had gone. And the family was too stunned to do anything—they just sat there thinking "No way! This can't be happening! This is too weird!" But it was true. All the food was gone.

The Breckenridges sat there and looked at the empty table. They looked at each other. Finally, Sarah, the youngest one, said, "Now what do we have to be thankful for? Our dinner is gone!" Everybody was about to cry (except Dad, who kept saying to himself, "I don't believe this! I don't believe this!").

Then Katy said, "Hey Mom—this reminds me of that time when we came home from soccer practice, and you said you were too stressed out to cook, so you took us to McDonald's, and we brought our hamburgers back and put them on the table, and then we went to get something, and the dog came and ate them up! Remember that? When we came back there was nothing on the table, just like now! It's kind of like that!"

Mom said, "Oh boy, do I remember that! I was so upset. That was terrible. How did we ever eat that night?"

Jimmy said, "And I remember the time when we were on that trip to see Grandma, and the car broke down and we had to spend two nights in a hotel in a town that we didn't even know the name of, and we had to eat in our hotel room!"

Dad said, "Oh, I remember that too. But what about the time when we climbed that trail to the top of the mountain at the park and then it began to rain! Remember how it took us two hours to get up but only 25 minutes to get down? Boy, were we running down that hill!"

Sarah said, "And remember when Jimmy and me—"

"Jimmy and I," said Mom.

"When Jimmy and I dressed up as a double ghost for Halloween and then couldn't remember whose candy was whose? And we fought over it and smushed the peanut butter cups in each other's hair? That was pretty funny."

And then Katy said, "And remember that summer when it was so hot, and we sprayed each other with the hose and then Dad came home from work and we sprayed him? That was really funny. I don't think Dad thought it was that funny, though."

They continued telling stories like these. They remembered the times they had gone places together and played games together, and the times they had gotten sick, and the times they had gotten well, and even the time when Katy let a chocolate bar melt on the front seat of the car and Mom sat on it. As they talked, Sarah began to think.

She said, "You know what? Even if we don't have our dinner, this is what we can be thankful for!"

And they all looked at her, and they stopped and smiled.

"Let's join hands," said Sarah.

And then Mom said, "For the love which flows in our family and for the love which arises even around an empty table, we are thankful." She lit the one candle that was still on the table.

And then they went out for pizza.

Some questions for you to think about:

- What are traditions? Describe a tradition from your family.

- What is your favorite part about the way you and your family celebrate Thanksgiving?

- How would you feel about celebrating Thanksgiving with a special breakfast (instead of a big meal at noon or suppertime)? Why?

- Can you remember something "bad" or unlucky that happened to you (or your family) that seems funny to you now?

- What are you most thankful for on any given day, not just on Thanksgiving?

Some things for you to do:

- Design a fancy menu that shows the kind of meal you and your family usually have at Thanksgiving or the kind you would like to have. Show it to someone outside your family and compare your usual menu with theirs.

- Make up a prayer or grace for Thanksgiving or for any mealtime.

- Through dance or creative movement, demonstrate the way the various Thanksgiving foods "walked" out the door: turkey, sweet potatoes, mashed potatoes, cranberry sauce, ice cream, and so on. Add music, if you want.

- Create a recipe for a Thanksgiving pizza.

- Make up your own nonsense story.

A Candle for Us

by Colleen M. McDonald

"**S**o you finally have your court date! You must be happy," said Sharon's teacher.

"I am," Sharon agreed, which was the truth . . . at least part of it.

Later the school nurse declared, "Connie Daniel's a fine person. You're a very lucky girl."

"I know," Sharon answered, trying her best to sound like she really meant it.

"Once you're adopted, no one will have to know about your real mom," Sharon's friend Megan explained. "You'll have a regular family, just like everyone else."

"Yeah?" thought Sharon. Right now she sure didn't feel like everyone else.

Sharon's biological mother, Roberta, had a drug problem. She often left Sharon home alone, rarely bought groceries, and didn't seem to care whether Sharon got to school. When Sharon was eight, the state had placed her in foster care—a temporary home—where she would be taken care of while Roberta got help. That's when Sharon came to live with Connie Daniels. Three years later, Roberta still couldn't take care of herself, much less Sharon. So Connie was going to adopt Sharon, which meant they had to see a judge.

As the court date got closer, Sharon and Connie started making special plans. They looked at adoption announcements in a card shop, but Sharon couldn't decide whether to buy one of the store's designs or make cards at home. Connie offered to take her shopping for new clothes for the big court date, but Sharon couldn't make up her mind about whether to choose something new or wear her Easter dress. Sharon and Connie talked about what they would do to celebrate the adoption, but Sharon couldn't choose between a family celebration and a bigger party that would include their friends.

Finally, Connie said to her, "You've been having so much trouble making these decisions, I'm wondering if you're not so sure you want to be adopted."

"Of course not!" Sharon answered quickly. "At least, I don't think so. I mean . . . oh, Mom, I'm so mixed up!"

"Happy and sad at the same time?" Connie asked.

"Yeah."

"Come here." Connie reached out to hold Sharon close. "I'll bet people are telling you how lucky you are, and you're thinking, 'So how come I'm getting adopted in the first place?'"

Sharon looked away but nodded.

"Maybe you're even wondering if things will ever change enough so you can be a regular kid like your friends. What would you say if I told you that I know what it's like to feel different, too?"

"You do? What do you mean?" asked Sharon.

"Well, I grew up thinking I'd be the kind of mom who has babies. But first I wanted to go to college. Then I started a job. I began seeing other women my age starting families, and I kept thinking it would happen to me, too, someday. After a while, I started getting worried. I'd watch my friends with their children and wonder why I was so unlucky."

"Like when I see other kids with their moms—and wonder how come I didn't get one who could take care of me?" Sharon asked.

"Something like that. I want you to know I understand if the idea of being adopted makes you feel sad and not just happy. It reminds you that you are not going back to live with your birth mom, and I know how much you wanted that. I feel sad things didn't work out the way you'd hoped."

Sharon and Connie sat quietly for a few minutes.

"Are you sad you didn't get your baby?" Sharon asked, finally.

"Yeah—sometimes. I've been waiting and hoping for a long time. And looking for a husband, too! But you know, I finally did get lucky—I found you!"

"And I found you," said Sharon, beginning to smile.

A few weeks later Sharon and Connie went to the mall. They went into a candle shop, and Connie invited Sharon to pick out a candle she liked. Sharon chose a green one. Connie found a blue one for herself, and they bought a third, a blue-green candle that both of them admired.

That night, after they'd cleared the dinner dishes, Connie put the three candles in the middle of the dining room table and turned the lights down low.

"Before we go to court tomorrow," Connie began, "I want to have a little ceremony."

Sharon kept her questions to herself and watched closely.

Striking a match, Connie lit the green candle and explained, "I light this candle for you, Sharon, for the family you've come from and for everyone who has loved you. For the happy and the sad times, the good luck and the bad luck, and for everything else that has made you the special person you are."

Connie paused, then lit the blue candle.

"I light this blue candle for myself—for the family I came from and for everyone who's loved me. For the happy and the sad times, the good luck and the bad luck, and for everything else that has made me the special person I am."

Connie paused again. Then she picked up her candle and asked Sharon to do the same with her own. The two of them, together, lit the blue-green candle that remained.

"Do you know what this last candle is for?" Connie asked her.

"You and me?" Sharon guessed.

"That's right—we light this candle for us—for the love that has joined us and for everyone who cares about us. For the happy and the sad times, the good luck and the bad luck that we will share together, from now on. For all that will make us a family and for everything that will make our family special."

"And for being together forever," Sharon added.

"Amen."

They watched the flames in silence for awhile. Then Sharon asked, "Mom, can we have our dessert now?"

Connie laughed.

"Coming right up. I love you Sharon. I love you very much."

"Yeah, Mama." Sharon smiled. "I know."

Some questions for you to think about:

- What makes a family? What do children need most from their families?

- How many different family groupings (adoptive, single parent, children living with grandparents, and so on) are represented in families you know?

- What do you know about foster care? Adoption?

- Can you remember a time when you felt happy and sad at the same time? If so, describe it. What kinds of events or experiences might make a person feel both happy and sad?

- What makes people love one another? What brings people closer together?

Some things for you to do:

- Draw a picture or write a story about Sharon and Connie's adoption-day celebration (a celebration between the two of them or with others).

- Write a poem, song, or rap, or make a poster or collage on the theme "love makes a family."

- Design a "Happy Adoption Day" card that Sharon or Connie might have given to one another, or write a letter from Sharon to Connie (or from Connie to Sharon) after they have seen the judge and become a "forever family."

- Imagine adults have to get a license before they can become parents. Create a list of questions for them to answer and tests they should be able to pass before they are judged ready to have or adopt children.

- Create your own candle-lighting ritual to celebrate a special event or relationship in your life.

Everyone
Must Be Free
to Search for
What Is True and
Right in Life

Grand-mother's Gift

by Colleen M. McDonald

The very first people—our great, great, great, great grandmother and grandfather—came out of the earth, growing out of the soil like a tulip or a grapevine or a weeping willow tree. But the earth they lived on had no plants.

The first woman and man blessed the earth and sang a song of thanksgiving for the gift of life. Then they walked around their home and explored for a time, scrambling up rocks, slipping through sand, splashing in rivers, and climbing toward the sky, on steep mountain cliffs. When they had enough they returned to the place where they had been born and settled down. In time they had children, their children had children, their grandchildren had children, and so on.

As more and more babies were born, the land started filling up. Women, men, and children spread farther and farther across the face of the earth, looking for open space they could call their own, and claiming territory toward the east and the west, the north and the south. At that time in the history of the world, no one ever died, and so the earth could only become more crowded.

Finally, when it seemed that the earth was holding almost as many people as could live together in peace, a great council was called in the place where the first humans had been born. The people decided they needed to stop having children.

In the months and years that followed, infants became children, children became teens, and teens became adults, until at last the feel of a newborn held securely in one's arms became only a memory. Until the sounds of cooing and babbling, of first words, and of baby talk faded away. Until the sight of girls' bodies rounding into womanhood, and boys' faces growing manly whiskers disappeared because everyone on earth had grown up.

Now, remember, at that time no one ever died, and so the first woman and man were still alive. One day, the woman began thinking aloud. "Life has been wonderful," she said to her husband. "I've climbed to points so high I could almost touch the stars. I've seen more twilights and dawns than I could possibly count. I've rocked and tended my babies, and their babies, and their babies. I'm ready to rest now." She turned to her husband. "Remember when our home was full of children?"

The man nodded.

"I miss them!" they both said at once.

"Yes," the woman continued. "I'm ready to give up my place on earth so that more children can come into this world."

"Give up your place on earth?" asked the man. "But where would you go?"

"I'd go back to where I came from—back into the earth."

"And then what? What will happen then?" the man wondered.

"I don't know," said the woman. "But the earth is our mother, and I am not afraid."

The woman sent out a call to her children and grandchildren and great grandchildren, who were scattered among the four corners of the earth. She told them what she was planning to do and asked them to come home.

The woman and the man and their many children gathered on the land, at the birth spot where the now-oldest humans had sprung up out of the soil. The family members shared news of what was happening to them now, told stories from their life together, and remembered precious moments long buried in forgetfulness. They laughed and they cried and they gave thanks for their time together. No one wanted to say good-bye to the woman, but they let her go, and she returned to the earth. And so, death came to the first human being.

Time passed. Nothing seemed to have changed until, one day, someone spotted a thin green curl springing out of the soil that had received the woman. In the days that followed, the curl grew longer and longer and sprouted more and more greenery. Tiny clumps, like closed fists, appeared, and then opened to display rainbow colors and give off a gentle perfume. The people had never seen anything like it! The plant bore delicate clusters, shiny and sweet. Humans, who had never before tasted fruit, delighted in this gift. "So this is what comes of dying!" they said. The plant finally withered, but its seeds brought new blossoms and more fruit in the season the people named "spring."

Reassured, more and more people followed the first woman and returned to the earth, making room so that babies were born once again. Children grew up accepting death, knowing their time would come one day, too.

And so death comes to each of us. The earth continues to call our bodies home. Spring still comes . . . and the flowers bloom.

Some questions for you to think about:

- How do you feel about death?
- What do you think happens when people die?
- Should people have a say in when and where they die? Why or why not? If yes, in what circumstances?
- How can you be helpful to someone who is dying?
- What can you do for friends or family after someone close to them has died?

Some things for you to do:

- Find the obituary section of a newspaper and see what kind of information goes into an obituary. Then write "the world's first obituary" for the main character in the story, adding as many details as you can. If you'd like, draw a "photograph" of her.
- Imagine what the first flower looked like. Use paint or markers and paper to show the design, or make a three-dimensional flower out of craft materials.

■ Find an interesting plant growing indoors or outdoors. Pretend this plant is the world's first plant. Imagine you have never seen a plant before and that words describing plant parts (for example, leaves, flowers) haven't been invented yet. How would you describe this plant? If you want, share this description with someone else and see if that person can guess what you're describing.

■ Illustrate an event in the story (your favorite part or something particularly interesting).

■ Pantomime (act out without words) the following parts of this story for others:

—The first woman telling her husband she plans to return to the earth

—The first man hearing this news

—A family member saying good-bye to the woman

—Someone discovering the first plant/flower/fruit

■ If you'd like, share the pantomimes with others who are familiar with the story, and ask them to guess what part of the story you're acting out.

A Little Jar Labeled Freedom

by Cynthia B. Johnson

Once upon a time, long, long ago, there was a Creator who had a hobby of making planets. The Creator took pride in making each one different. One day she looked at a gap in the solar system and said, "I think I'll make a planet to go over there. Let me think . . . how will I make *this* one?" She sat and looked out into the vast reaches of swirling matter and thought long and hard about creating another planet in her collection. She had a very large closet in which she had rows and rows of shelves with little jars and envelopes on them.

To begin, she took a large glass jar down from a shelf and started adding ingredients to her planet—a pinch of this, a pinch of that. In went daffodils and puppies and pizza. She added ladybugs and butterflies . . . and fire ants, just to make her planet interesting. She poured in lots of liquid from the jar marked "Oceans and Seas" and from the jar marked "Clear Lakes" and slowly poured in more liquid from a jar labeled "Waterfalls." She smiled and added just a dash from the jar labeled "Mud Puddles." She decided to shake in a sample from all her boxes labeled "Human Beings." She combined people of all sizes and shapes and ages, many colors of skin and hair, many different kinds of noses, and many different interests and skills. Over all the people she sprinkled some powder called "Change," so that the people would change in size and age, interests and skills. "That will make this new planet interesting," she mused. "I'm glad I thought to do this."

She looked in the bin called "Moods and Emotions," wondering whether she should add a little or a lot. She started with love, adding more than two cups, and then, with a mischievous smile, she closed her eyes and reached into the jar labeled "Miscellaneous," where there were bits and pieces of Sadness and Courage, Loneliness and Happiness, Regret and Hope. She shook in some schools and universities. She shook in some churches and temples so that people could come together to remember what is important in life.

She added comfortable shoes and blue jeans, and warm coats and bathing suits. From her bottle called "Smells," she dropped in a pinch of Hyacinth, a pinch of Just Baked Chocolate Chip Cookies, a pinch of Freshly Mowed Grass, and—just to make it interesting—a pinch of Skunk. She amused herself for days and days, designing her new planet. Finally, she was almost done. Almost.

There was one more ingredient she wanted to add. She turned her closet upside down looking for the one special jar she remembered that she had but that she had never used before. Finally, she found it behind a jar tagged "Kalimavda" (whatever that is). She carefully lifted down a little jar labeled "Freedom." This time she read the description. The label said, "This compound will aid in the ability to make choices, to choose one thing instead of another thing. Use cautiously because the choices made will have consequences." The Creator smiled as she measured out twice the maximum recommended dosage. She said to herself, "This will make it especially interesting."

She held the open jar in her hands, slowly turning it as she looked down into it. A soft chuckle rumbled out of her mouth and into the jar. A tear trickled down her cheek and into the jar also. She leaned over and blew in her warm breath. And then she screwed on the cover and flung the jar away into the star-speckled darkness. It landed just where she intended—about 93 million miles from her favorite Sun. The Creator watched her planet settle into its new home. She thought, "What a nice piece of work! I hope they'll appreciate all the special things I did to make their planet interesting." Then she sat down with a good book, a bowl of popcorn, and some Kalimavda.

Some questions for you to think about:

- What decisions or choices have you made that led to something bad happening?
- What other bad things happen in the world as a consequence of people's choices?

- What are some examples of bad decisions that hurt people? What decisions or choices have you made that led to something good happening?

- What freedoms or choices should people your age be allowed to have or make? Explain. What freedoms or choices should people your age not be allowed to have or make? Why not?

Some things for you to do:

- Create a recipe for planet Earth. Include a list of ingredients and step-by-step instructions.

- Using paint, play dough, or recyclables, design your own planet. Give it a name. Describe how it is similar to other planets, and what makes it unique.

- Write your own myth

  –describing how the world came to be; OR

  –explaining why bad things happen; OR

  –answering some other question about why something in the world is the way it is.

- Compose a rap, song (using a familiar melody), or poem about good and/or bad things on earth.

- Create a magazine/newspaper, radio, or television ad for kalimavda. Consider including music and/or a jingle, sound effects, or props.

Answer Mountain

by Sarah E. Skwire

Long ago and far away, or yesterday and just around the corner, or maybe somewhere halfway in between, there was a town that sat, quiet and content, tucked into the shadow of a mountain. And carved on the side of that mountain, big and tall so no one could miss them, were the words, "THE ANSWER IS NO." No one knew where the words came from or why they were there. They'd just always been there.

But, oh my goodness, the people who lived in that town cuddled into that mountain were glad to have those words there. Because whenever the townspeople had a question, all they had to do was to look up the mountain and read it. The answer was always "NO."

Making decisions was very simple, and life went on smoothly and easily in the town cuddled into the mountain . . . until one day. Now, on that particular day, Ma Custus was about to make dinner for her family. And she just couldn't decide—because sometimes you can't—whether to make stew or steak, pasta or potatoes, dumplings or doughnuts, so she went out into the yard.

"Should I make liver for dinner tonight?" she asked, and looked up at the mountain.

And the mountain said, "THE ANSWER IS NO."

"All right. I knew that, really. Nobody is crazy about liver. But should I maybe make steak for dinner?"

And the mountain said, "THE ANSWER IS NO."

"Should I make chicken?"

And the mountain said, "THE ANSWER IS NO."

"Should I make tacos or tofu? Baked beans or broccoli? Pork chops or popcorn?"

The mountain said nothing but "THE ANSWER IS NO."

Ma Custus asked more questions until the sun disappeared behind the mountain. She kept on asking questions until the sun came up around the other way. And all the mountain ever said was "THE ANSWER IS NO." Because Ma couldn't get an answer that was any kind of answer, she and her family went all night and all the next day and all the next night without dinner.

Finally, Ma just gave up and made liver anyway—even though the mountain said no, and even though everyone hated liver—because liver was the first thing she'd thought of.

But Ma Custus had had enough. She glared at the mountain, stamped her foot, and shook her fist. "Why is the answer always 'NO'? Why can't you just say 'YES' for once?"

Ma turned around and stomped away to ring the town bell and call a town meeting.

Well, when that bell rang, the whole town came running. From the oldest man with the longest beard to the youngest kids who still needed carrying, no one would miss a town meeting. They all came, and they all listened carefully as Ma Custus told her story.

"Seems to me," she said, "that we've got a problem. That mountain just isn't helping us like it should. Seems to me it would be nice if it would say 'YES' for a while."

The townsfolk knew Ma Custus had a point, but they didn't much like this idea—changing something that had been the same for so long. But after they thought and then thought some more, they finally nodded solemnly. The mountain would have to be re-carved.

Mason Sharp, the stone carver, nodded along with the rest of them. He scratched his nose, adjusted his cap, and slowly gazed up the length of the mountain.

Then he cleared his throat and said, in his gravelly voice, "Looks to me like I could do the carving, if that's all right with all of you."

And so it was. Mason spent the next two weeks up on the side of the mountain, chiseling and chipping and carving away, and coming down only when it got too dark to see. And when he was done, the mountain said, "THE ANSWER IS YES."

Mason rang the bell to call the town together, and once again they all came running. From the oldest woman with the whitest hair to the youngest kids who still needed carrying, they all wanted to see the new sign, and they all wanted to cheer for the stone carver and all his hard work.

Ma Custus, who had started all of this, came right up to the front of the crowd. She figured she ought to be the person to ask the first question of this new and different mountain, since she'd discovered the problem with the old one. She stepped right up to the foot of the mountain, looked way up to the top, and asked, "Should I make liver for dinner tonight?"

And the mountain said, "THE ANSWER IS YES."

Well, now, Ma Custus almost fell over with surprise.

"But Pa Custus told me he'd never forgive me if I served liver again, and all my kids threatened to hide in the barn for a week. Should I really serve liver?"

And the mountain said, "THE ANSWER IS YES."

The townspeople began to grumble. They didn't like the sound of this. Ma Custus's family grumbled the loudest.

"But, well, I can't," Ma said. "I mean, I just can't serve liver again. I promised I wouldn't! Are you telling me I should break my promise?"

The mountain said, "THE ANSWER IS YES."

The grumbling got louder. And Ma Custus, well, she glared at the mountain again, stamped her foot and shook her fist, and she turned to the townspeople and said, "This just isn't right! This just can't be right! What are we going to do?"

Once again, the townsfolk put on their thinking caps. Everyone thought: Ma Custus, Pa Custus, and all the Custus kids (who probably thought the hardest of all, because they were worried about the liver—very worried). Finally, the smallest but one of the Custus kids piped up.

"Why does there have to be just one answer? Can't we have more?"

The townspeople gasped. No one had ever thought of such a thing before. They mumbled and grumbled and talked among themselves. Finally they decided that the mountain ought to say, "THE ANSWER IS SOMETIMES YES AND SOMETIMES NO AND SOMETIMES WAIT AND SEE AND SOMETIMES I JUST DON'T KNOW."

Mason the stone carver, who had been listening to all of this talk, cleared his throat, scratched his nose, adjusted his cap, and said, "I think I can do it. I don't mind—not really—even if I did just finish carving in the new change. But, well, it's going to take a lot of time, and I can't work all day long like I did the last time. How about if I work on it when I can, and we'll hang us up some kind of sign on the mountain that lets people know that the answer is coming?"

And so it was.

The funny thing was that, for a little while, Mason worked on the mountain every day. And for a little while, everyone in town waited eagerly to see the new answer. But soon, the stonemason got tired of climbing the mountain every day and everyone else got tired of waiting, and they all started asking each other questions and helping everyone else find answers that seemed to fit. The townspeople realized that different questions usually had different answers, that sometimes the same question had more than one answer, and that there were many more answers than they had imagined. And all of that was fine with them.

After a while they thought that maybe the answer the mountain was giving them right then, just as it was, was better and more sensible than any other answer it had given. And so they left it as it was.

And the mountain said, "THE ANSWER IS UNDER CONSTRUCTION."

Some questions for you to think about:

- What are some different ways people can go about finding an answer to a question?

- Imagine that your parents always said "yes" to you. In what ways would that be bad? Now imagine that they always said "no." Why might that be a problem?

- What are some questions that have more than one good answer?

- What are some questions that no one can answer for sure?

- If you could be sure someone could give you the right answer to any question, what would you want to know?

Some things for you to do:

- Use clay or recyclables to make your own "Answer Mountain."

- Choose a question that has many different answers and use it to make a word collage: In large letters, write the question on a piece of paper or poster-board, then write as many answers as you can, using different colors, lettering, and kinds of ink (such as markers, paints, glitter pens) for different answers.

- Ask the members of your family, "What shall we make for dinner tonight?" or imagine each person's answer, given what you know about her or his favorite foods. Then come up with a menu that will appeal to everyone. Work together to shop for the ingredients and cook the meal. If you want, do the same thing with breakfast and/or lunch.

- Write five or more questions (or riddles) on index cards (one question per card) and then write the answers to those questions on additional cards. Separate the question cards from the answer cards. Mix up each pile. Draw a question card and get a wacky response by drawing a mixed-up answer card. (For more fun, play this game with a group.)

- Obtain a copy of *Highlights* magazine and find the column called "Dear Highlights." Read the problems and the answers/advice that have been sent in by readers. What do you think of the suggested solutions? Do you have other advice? Write a letter to *Highlights*, asking for advice about a problem you have or giving advice to a reader who has asked for it.

Grady
Asks
Why

by Colleen M. McDonald

Grady the ground hog and her family lived in a hole in the ground. Every fall, they would feast on berries, clover, and flower stems until everyone was quite round. Then, sometime in October, they would take a few good whiffs of the crisp autumn air before disappearing into their burrow. They would stay there, mostly sleeping, for about five months.

Every few weeks Grady would wake up.

"Is it time yet? Is it time yet?" she would ask her mother.

"Go back to sleep. I'll wake you when it's time."

When it was time, the whole family would be up before the sun. (Not that they could tell what the sun was doing.) They wouldn't eat breakfast—they never ate much of anything while they were hibernating—

but they would yawn and stretch and get their blood pumping a little—just in case. And they would all watch the clock.

"Good luck, Dad," Grady would call, as Father began climbing up to the burrow's entrance. Everyone would listen hard, imagining the scene that would greet him when he stepped outside, at precisely 7:25 A.M.

If the day was clear and bright, Father would announce, "The sun is out today. Winter's here to stay."

Then, no matter how pleasant and warm the day might be, Father would step back in the burrow right away. Mother would say, "Six more weeks of winter," and everyone would soon be back to sleep.

If the sky was grey and cloudy, Father would say, "The sun is gone today. Spring is on the way."

That would be the signal for Mother, Grady, and little Phil to come out of the burrow and spend the rest of the day in the fresh air—and sometimes the rain, or sleet, or snow.

On one of these mornings, Father returned to the burrow, having spotted the sun rising in a cloudless sky.

"Back to bed, everyone," Mother instructed.

"Now wait a minute," said Grady. "I haven't seen the sun in months. Why do we always stay inside on bright and sunny Ground Hog Days?"

Mother and Father were silent for a minute. Finally, Father said, "I don't know, Grady. It's been that way as long as I can remember. It's our tradition—something passed down to us from my father's family, and his father's family, and his father's family, and so on.

Just like Ground Hog Day is always on February second, not February first or February third. Just like I step out of the hole precisely at 7:25 in the morning, not twelve noon or ten o'clock at night."

"But it doesn't make sense to me," said Grady. "We go outside and freeze our butts when it's damp and dreary, and we stay inside when we could be having fun in the sun. Do you think Grandpa could give me an answer?"

"Perhaps," said Mother. "But it's time to go to sleep, now. I'll wake you next month."

■   ■   ■

Six weeks later, on a windy March day, Grady found Grandpa at work up on a hill, using his sharp claws to peel bark off a tree.

"Grandpa," said Grady as she chewed on the bark her grandfather had given her, "why do ground hogs always stay inside on bright and sunny Ground Hog days?"

"Can't say I've ever thought much about that," Grandpa answered. "That's just what ground hogs do. Does there have to be a reason?"

"Of course there does! And I want to find out what it is," declared Grady.

"Then why don't you ask my mother?" suggested Grandpa. "She's one of the oldest, wisest ground hogs around."

Grady tracked down Great Grandmother and asked her. "Why, I haven't thought about that in years," Great Grandmother replied. "You know, when I was just about your age, I asked my Great Grandmother the same question. And she told me the story of the Sun Spook."

"Tell me," begged Grady.

"Well, it seems that, long ago, one of our great, great, great, great grandfather ground hogs met up with a dark, flat ghost of a creature, as soon as he stepped outside on a sunny Ground Hog Day."

"The Sun Spook?" asked Grady.

"Yes. It darted under his feet and stuck to his heels like glue. He tried to run away from it, but it slid along the ground right with him. So Great Grandfather scurried back into his burrow, and the Sun Spook disappeared."

"A dark, flat ghost?" Grady thought for a moment. Then she smiled. "Great Grandma, I think I have my answer."

Back at home Grady told her family the story of their long-ago Great Grandfather and his adventure with the Sun Spook.

"You see, in the olden days," she explained, "ground hogs were afraid of their own shadows!"

Everyone laughed.

"But we know better than that. A shadow's no Sun Spook!" Grady turned to her parents. "So why can't we go outside today?"

"I don't know," said Father. "We've never done it that way before."

"Please? I promise I'll come in and go right to bed when Mother calls."

Father looked at Mother; Mother nodded.

"All right," Father agreed. "I guess we can give it a try."

"Great!" said Grady. "But before I go, I have just one more question: Why is it always the father ground hog who goes out to look for spring on Ground Hog Day?"

Some questions for you to think about:

- How does Grady's dad explain the reason behind their Ground Hog Day traditions? Why do you think it is hard for him to change the way they celebrate the holiday?

- What is Grady's question at the end of the story? (What does she really want to know?)

- Why do we have holidays like Ground Hog Day that help us celebrate spring?

- What do you think is true about this story? (What facts are included that tell you something about real ground hogs?)

- What "why" questions would you like to ask?

Some things for you to do:

- Search the Web for "Ground Hog Day." See what you can find out about the origin of the holiday and the real habits of ground hogs.

- Create your own holiday to celebrate the beginning of spring, some other season, or a kind of weather. When would it be, and how would you celebrate it? Consider food, decorations, games, stories, music, and special activities.

- Turn on a slide, overhead, or filmstrip projector in a darkened room, to make a "light stage." Experiment with different kinds of shadows you can make with your fingers, hands, other body parts, and objects. Make some that look scary. Choose one that is particularly interesting and trace it onto a large piece of newsprint. Decorate the shadow/shape with markers.

■ Write five or more questions that begin with "why" on index cards (one question per card) and then write the answers to those questions on additional cards. Separate the question cards from the answer cards. Mix up each pile. Draw a question card and get a wacky response by drawing a mixed up answer card. (For more fun, play this game with a group.)

■ Write a myth about why we have different seasons (or different kinds of weather) or a story about what it would be like to live in the dark and not see the sun for several months.

It Is Our
Responsibility
to Work for a
Peaceful, Fair,
and Free World

The Children's Crusade

by Kate Rohde

What are we going to do?" asked Martin Luther King, Jr., the well-known American civil rights leader, as he sat with his friends at a meeting in the Sixteenth Street Baptist Church in Birmingham, Alabama. Martin, who was trying to lead the black people of Birmingham in their struggle to end segregation, was worried that he and his friends were going to fail in their mission. Nevertheless, he rose from his chair at the front of the group.

"Who will demonstrate with me tomorrow in a brave attempt to end segregation? Who will risk going to jail for the cause?"

Often, four hundred people would show up for meetings like this one, but only thirty-five or so would volunteer to protest, and not all of these volunteers would show up the next day for the protest march. Those who did would gather downtown and parade through the streets, carry signs, chant, and sing, sending the message that segregation had to end.

In Martin's day, segregation meant that black people were not allowed to do the same things or go to the same places as white people. Black people couldn't go to most amusement parks, swimming pools, parks, hotels, or restaurants. They had to go to different schools that weren't as nice as the schools for white kids. They had to use separate drinking fountains, and they could get in big trouble for drinking out of fountains marked for white people. They weren't allowed to use the same bathrooms; many times, there was no bathroom at all that they could use. They weren't allowed to try on clothes before they bought them, like white people could.

Black people didn't think that was fair, and some white people agreed with them. In the 1950s and 1960s, many thousands of people worked to end segregation. But in many places, especially in the southern part of the United States, segregation was the law—and if black people tried to go somewhere they weren't supposed to go, they could get arrested, beaten, and even killed. In the spring of 1963, Martin Luther King went to Birmingham, Alabama, one of the largest and most heavily segregated cities in the south, to bring people together to change this law.

You see, the people were very scared. The sheriff in Birmingham was named Bull Connor. And black people didn't know what Bull Connor might do to them if he caught them protesting. Martin Luther King had already been in jail once, and others were afraid to follow him. Besides, they weren't sure protesting would do any good.

Martin, seeing that no one answered his call, again tried to inspire the group. "The struggle will be long," he said. "We must stand up for our rights as human beings. Who will demonstrate with me, and if necessary, be ready to go to jail for it?"

There was a pause, and then a whole group of people stood up. Someone gasped. All the people who had stood up were children. The adults told them to sit down, but they didn't.

Martin Luther King thanked the children and told them he appreciated their offer but that he couldn't ask them to go to jail. They still wouldn't sit down. They wanted to help.

That night, Martin talked with a close group of friends about the events of the day. "What are we going to do?" he asked. "The only volunteers we got were children. We can't have a protest with children!" Everyone nodded, except Jim Bevel. "Wait a minute," said Jim. "If they want to do it, I say bring on the children."

"But they are too young!" the others said. Then Jim asked, "Are they too young to go to segregated schools?"

"No!"

"Are they too young to be kept out of amusement parks?"

"No!"

"Are they too young to be refused a hamburger in a restaurant?"

"No!" said the others.

"Then they are not too young to want their freedom." That night, they decided that any child old enough to join a church was old enough to march.

The children heard about this decision and told their friends. When the time came for the march, a thousand children, teenagers, and college students gathered. The sheriff arrested them and put them in jail. The next day even more kids showed up—some of their parents and relatives too, and even more the next day and the next day. Soon lots of adults joined in. Finally, a thousand children were locked up together in a "children's jail," and there was no more room for anyone else.

Sheriff Connor had done awful things to try to get the children and the other protesters to turn back. He had turned loose big police dogs and allowed them to bite people. He had turned on fire hoses that were so strong, the force of the water could strip the bark off trees. He had ordered the firefighters to point the hoses at the little kids and roll them right down the street. People all over the country and all over the world saw the pictures of the dogs, the fire hoses, and the children, and they were furious.

Now the white people of Birmingham began to worry. All over the world people were saying bad things about their town. Even worse, everyone was afraid to go downtown to shop because of the fire hoses and the dogs. So they decided they might have to change things. A short time later, the black people and the white people of Birmingham made an agreement to desegregate the city and let everyone go to the same places.

Today, when people tell this story, many talk about Martin Luther King. But we should also remember the thousands of brave children and teenagers whose courage helped to defeat Bull Connor and end segregation in Birmingham, Alabama, and the rest of the United States.

Some questions for you to think about:

- Why do you think the adults finally agreed to let the children march?

- Why did Sheriff Connor act the way he did?

- How might your life be different if you had been born of another race?

- How would you define "fairness"?

- What can children do to work for change?

Some things for you to do:

- Choose one of the following scenes to act out (or write the scene as a short play):

  –A meeting at the church. Martin is trying to convince people to protest but most are afraid

  –A child trying to persuade his/her mom to let him/her protest

  –A policeman bringing news of the children's march to Sheriff Connor

- Imagine you are one of the children about to participate in the protest. Write a prayer or page in a diary sharing how you feel

  –the night before the protest

  –the night after the protest

- Check the newspaper for stories about protests and for photos of protesters. Where do the people live and what are the rules or laws they are trying to change?

■ Choose a rule at school, church, home, or elsewhere that you believe is unfair and would like to change. (Think carefully about whether the rule is truly unfair or just a rule you don't like.) What do you think started the rule? Why would some people argue it's a good rule? Why do you think it should be changed? How could you go about trying to change it? Before going ahead with a plan for change, talk over your ideas with a friend or family member and see if s/he thinks you have a good case.

■ Draw a picture or make a poster showing as many different kinds of people as you can think of getting along or working together.

The Evil Wizard

by Joshua Searle-White

This the story of an Evil Wizard and a girl named Esmeralda.

Esmeralda was a pretty normal nine-year-old girl except that for several years she had been on adventures all around the world, saving all kinds of people and animals from the clutches of the Evil Wizard. And the Evil Wizard was, well, evil. He was completely mean and rotten. Once, he stole a whole forest of animals and put them in cages in a cave underneath the ocean. Esmeralda had to save them. Once, the Evil Wizard stole a spaceship and went to the planet of the Garbles and tried to start a war there—he tried to get all the yellow-striped Garbles to kill the green-striped Garbles. Esmeralda had to stop him. And once, he went to Shangri-La, a place way up in the Himalayan Mountains where everybody is happy all the time and where nobody does anything except ride merry-go-rounds and water-ski and eat chocolate, and tried to wreck the fun and make everyone miserable. Esmeralda had to catch him and put him in jail. Esmeralda had spent a lot of her time chasing the Evil Wizard around the world, into space, under the oceans, up the mountains, and she had caught him every time.

But as many times as Esmeralda could stop the Evil Wizard from doing terrible things, he kept doing more. As many times as she could put him in jail, he broke out. It was very, very frustrating, but Esmeralda persisted because, after all, these creatures and people needed to be saved.

Then one summer day Esmeralda decided to go on a trip of her own. All her other adventures had started when the Evil Wizard had caused trouble somewhere. This time she was going on an adventure all by herself. It was a Saturday, and she was going to climb to the top of a mountain—a mountain she had wanted to climb for a long time. She got her backpack, her magic hat, her binoculars, some food, and some extra socks, and she headed off along the trail.

As she walked along she was enjoying the smells and the sun and the leaves. But she hadn't been walking for ten minutes when whom should she see, sitting on the path ahead of her, but—you guessed it—the Evil Wizard, dressed in his gloomy robe and grinning at her. "What is *he* doing here?" she said to herself. "I fight and fight and *fight* this guy, and every time I think I finally have him put away, he's back again. I can't believe it!" And just as she thought this, the Evil Wizard darted off the path and into the forest. Esmeralda ran after him, thinking, "This is it. This time he is not getting away.

I'm going to catch him, and when I do, I'm going to put him where he will *never* come out again. I don't ever want to see his ugly face again."

Esmeralda ran and ran, dodging trees, climbing up hills, jumping over streams. Finally, as the Evil Wizard ran around an enormous boulder, Esmeralda climbed on top of it and jumped off, landing right on top of him. He flailed around and tried to escape, but Esmeralda didn't lift weights for nothing, and he was overpowered. And Esmeralda thought to herself, "This is *finally* it. I'm going to put him where he will *never* get out." She looked around, and right there, next to the boulder, was a hole in the ground. She dragged the Evil Wizard over to the hole and stuffed him in. Then she looked around and spied a small rock underneath the boulder. She kicked that rock out of the way, and the boulder rolled right over the hole, sealing the Evil Wizard in.

"Phew!" she gasped. "He's trapped now. He's never coming out. And I am FREE!" Esmeralda turned and walked back to the trail, picked up her backpack, and started off again when she heard a sound behind her. She stopped. Slowly, she turned around, and there was the Evil Wizard, on top of a log, staring at her. Esmeralda threw herself onto the ground, pounded her fists, and kicked her feet.

"That's impossible! You can't be here," she cried. "How did you manage to escape *again?*" Then she thought, "I shouldn't have just put him in a hole—I should have dropped him off a cliff and let him tumble onto the rocks. I should have taken him to the ocean and let him get eaten by sharks!" And then she stopped herself. "What am I *saying?* I'm starting to sound like him, not me." She looked at the Evil Wizard. He looked at the trail, and she looked at her watch. She realized that she'd spent most of the day trying to conquer the Evil Wizard and nearly forgotten about her climb up the mountain.

Esmeralda thought about that for a minute, and then she realized something else. "Maybe trying to get rid of him isn't the answer. If I wait to go on my adventure until I get rid of him, I might never get *anywhere*. Something has to change."

"Okay, Evil Wizard," she called out to him when she'd made her decision. "This is it. I'm going on this journey, and I'm not going to let you take over. I won't let you do anything evil, but I'm not taking off after you just because you decide to show up. This is *my* adventure. If you want to come along, okay, I'll have to deal with you, but you'll also have to deal with *me*."

Esmeralda took a deep breath, shouldered her backpack, and proceeded up the mountain. And the Evil Wizard? Well, he looked around, hopped off his log, and went after her, but *she* continued in the lead.

You may wonder, did Esmeralda make it up the mountain? Well, *that* story will have to wait for another day.

Some questions for you to think about:

- Who was your favorite character in the story? How are you like that character? How are you different?
- Why do you think the Evil Wizard was so evil?

- What made Esmeralda so strong and brave?

- Have you ever had a problem that didn't go away, no matter how hard you tried? What was it, and what did you do about it?

- Like Esmeralda climbing the mountain, are there adventures you look forward to having some day?

Some things for you to do:

- Imagine what the Evil Wizard looks like. Create a mask of his face.

- Make yourself a magic hat like the one Esmeralda took with her on her journey. Describe how it works and what it does.

- Act out the story after making up a different ending.

- Write a story or draw a picture about Esmeralda and the Mountain (the next chapter) or your own adventure.

Spite Fences

by Paul Beckel

Not too long ago, four neighbors were living together in peace and harmony. They liked to get together to play and to sing and to have barbecue. (They grilled out so often, in fact, that one of the neighbors planted a grill permanently in her backyard.) These friends always liked to eat hamburgers at their barbecues. Some would have cheese on their burgers. Others preferred just lettuce. A few loved to pour on globs of steak sauce. They liked the fact they all could eat their hamburgers any way they wanted.

One day the neighbor with the grill got a job in another city and had to move away. As the remaining friends waved goodbye,[1] they shed a few tears[2] because they were sure that no one would ever be able to take the place of that friend who'd built the neighborhood grill.

82

A few days later a new neighbor moved in. The others watched carefully[3] as the new neighbor moved in her things. They were delighted when she set up a grill that evening and began to heat up some coals. She was going to fit right in. But wait a minute—where was the hamburger? The stranger placed something soft and flabby onto the grill, and as it cooked it gave off an odor that was too unfamiliar to be pleasant. "Pew!"[4] said the other neighbors. Everyone ran into their houses and locked the doors.

The new neighbor soon came around knocking[5] on doors to invite everyone to dinner. But the others pretended they weren't home. They called each other on the phone and said, "We've got to get rid of that new neighbor or at least make sure her awful cooking smells[6] don't pollute *our* backyards."

They decided they would build fences around their backyards, fences so tall that no awful smells[7] would ever reach over them, fences so high that sunbeams wouldn't shine into her windows or nourish her grass. Maybe—if they were lucky—the new neighbor would move away when her house got dark and her grass turned brown. Perhaps then the right kind of person would move in.

And so these neighbors put up their fences—fences[8] that prevented even the tiniest[9] beam of light from squeezing through. Then the neighbors waited to see what would happen. Unfortunately, they could no longer attend the barbecues they had so enjoyed, but at least they didn't have to put up with that strange smell any more.

They'd been in such a hurry to put up the fences, however, that they soon had a number of problems. First of all, the fences were about as attractive as a clump of weeds, and other neighbors on the block started complaining. Second, the fences were so humongous that they were very hard to paint.[10] Finally, the fences were so heavy that they started to sag[11] after a while.

One day the fences just collapsed with a **BOOM**.[12] The neighbors cautiously came out of their houses to see what had happened. The new neighbor was nowhere in sight. "Oh no!" they gasped. "What if she's hurt?"

Well, she wasn't hurt. *She was gone!* Now, they hadn't seen her since the day she moved in, so for all they knew she might have moved out weeks ago! The neighbors realized they had gotten what they wanted, but they weren't happy about that. In fact, they were starting to think they'd made a big mistake.

That's all of the story I know. Help me figure out an ending.

NOTES: *This story includes motions you can use to make it more dramatic and give the audience a way of helping you act it out. These movements are noted.*

1. *Wave your hand.*
2. *With fingertips, "draw" tears coming down your cheeks.*
3. *Use your hands to form "spy glasses" around your eyes.*
4. *Hold your nose.*
5. *Pretend to knock with your fist.*
6. *Hold your nose.*
7. *Hold your nose.*
8. *Raise your arms high over your head and touch your fingertips together.*

9. *Bring your thumb and forefinger close together, with a tiny space in between.*

10. *Rub the back of your neck.*

11. *Let your head drop onto your chest.*

12. *Stomp your foot.*

Some questions for you to think about:

■ What else besides building fences could the neighbors have done to solve their problem?

■ What have you learned from someone who was/is very different from you in some way (for example, different in religion, race, culture, or age)?

■ Are there fences where you live? If so, what purpose do they serve? In what ways are fences beneficial? How can fences be harmful?

■ Like the new neighbor in the story, have you ever felt unwelcome? Where? What did you do about it?

■ Would you describe your own neighborhood as friendly or unfriendly? Why?

■ What can you do to be friendly to someone new to your neighborhood, class, or other group to which you belong?

Some things for you to do:

■ Design a "friendly" or an "unfriendly" fence. Use odds and ends such as cardboard tubes, Popsicle sticks, toothpicks, pipe cleaners, plastic straws, yarn, and fabric. Explain where you might put up such a fence.

- Find two other people to make a group of three. Figure out three ways in which all of you are alike and three ways in which you are different.
- Act out the story from the new neighbor's point of view.
- Draw a picture of the fences in this story.
- Write a poem on the subject of "Fences," "Neighbors," or "Differences" as follows:

   ‒One word: Title (noun)

   ‒Two words: Describing the word you just chose (adjective)

   ‒Three words: Actions describing the subject (words ending in "ing")

   ‒One sentence: Description of what you think or how you feel about the subject

   ‒One word: Repeating the first word or naming something similar to the first word (synonym)

- Add to the story by writing about what you think might happen next.

What If Nobody Forgave?

by Barbara Marshman

In a land far away, a wise old man who knew a great deal about people because he traveled from place to place arrived at a strange village. In this town all the people were carrying what seemed to be great bundles on their backs. They couldn't look around very well, and they never looked up because of the heavy burdens they carried.

Puzzled, the wise old man finally stopped a young fellow. "My good man, I am a stranger to your land and am fascinated by these large bundles you all carry about but never seem to put down. What is their purpose?"

"Oh, these," answered the young fellow in a matter-of-fact way. "These are our grudges."

"My," said the wise old man, "that's a lot of grudges to collect at your age!"

"Oh, they're not all mine. Most of them were passed down in my family." The young fellow heaved a weary sigh. "See that man over there? I have quite a load of grudges against his family. His great, great grandfather called mine a horse thief when they both wanted to be elected mayor."

The wise man looked around and shook his head sadly. "You all look so unhappy. Is there no way to get rid of these burdens?"

"We've forgotten how," said the young fellow, shifting his load a little. "You see, at first we were proud of our grudges. Tourists came from miles around. But after a few years, Grudgeville became a dreary place. Nobody came. And we had forgotten how to stop holding our grudges."

"If you really want to get rid of those grudges," said the wise old man, "I think I know five magic words that will do the trick."

"You do?" asked the fellow hopefully. "That would be a miracle. I'll go and have the mayor call the people of Grudgeville together." And off he went, as fast as his grudges would let him.

The mayor lost no time calling the people to the village square. The mayor and the wise old man stood on a platform where they could see all the hunched-over villagers.

When the people had quieted down, the mayor said, "Good people of Grudgeville, a wonderful thing has happened! A very wise stranger has come into our town. He says he can tell us the magic words that will rid us of these grudges we have carried for generations. How many of you would like to be able to straighten up, have your grudges disappear, look at the world in a whole new way? Listen to the wise words of our visitor, then, and do as he tells you."

"My friends, these are simple words, yet some people find them hard to say," said the wise stranger. "I think you have the courage to speak them. The trick is that you must say them to each other and truly mean them. The first two words are 'I'm sorry.' Can you say them? The other three are 'I forgive you.' Can you say that? Now say these words to each other."

There was a long pause, then a low grumble from the townspeople. First one person, and then another, said the words. Soon they were all saying them to each other—quietly at first and then louder. And then—would you believe it? Just like the wise man predicted, the grudges disappeared! What joy there was in the town. People were heard saying, "Look how those trees have grown!" and "Is that you, Jim? How good to see your face!"

There was dancing in the streets that day, and it wasn't long before the mayor changed the name of the town to Joytown.

NOTE: *This story was developed for use with hand puppets or flannel board. The suggested background is the facade of a town hall, with a sign reading GRUDGEVILLE. The sign should have holes punched in either end, through which pins hold it to the board so it can be turned over at the end, to read JOY-TOWN. For the flannel board, cardboard figures can be joined at the waist and held onto the board with folded masking tape.*

Some questions for you to think about:

- Do you think it's a good idea to make people apologize when they've done something wrong? Why or why not?

- How can you tell when an apology is real—when the person making it is truly sorry?

- What are some ways, besides apologizing, that you can show someone you're sorry?

- Can you remember a time, not too long ago, when you apologized to someone? What were the circumstances and how did you feel? When has someone apologized to you? How did you feel then?

- Are you able to forgive a person who has hurt you but isn't willing to apologize? If so, how do you do it?

Some things for you to do:

- Create a dance showing townspeople getting rid of their burdens.

- Make an "I'm sorry" card for someone to whom you want to apologize.

- Imagine what a grudge, or a bundle of grudges, looks like. What would you see when you opened the bundle? Use paints, clay, or recyclables to make a grudge or bundle of grudges.

■ Along the left-hand side of a piece of paper, spell out "MAGIC WORDS" diagonally. Using "I" as the beginning of the first word, write, "I'm sorry." Use the other letters to spell out other "magic words" we can use to solve a disagreement or make up after a quarrel. Then copy the whole thing onto a larger piece of paper and make a poster by adding pictures.

■ Pretend you are a reporter doing a story about the town that changed its name from "Grudgeville" to "Joytown." Come up with a headline and then write a news story about how this change came to be. Draw a "photo" to go along with the story.

All People Should Have a Voice and a Vote About Things That Concern Them

Susan Goes to Work

by Colleen M. McDonald

One hundred years ago in America, women were not allowed to do many of the things that men could; they could not even vote for the president of the country. One woman, Susan B. Anthony, thought that women should have the same rights as men. She worked hard to change the laws and eventually became famous as an important activist for women's rights. But when Susan was twelve years old, no one knew that she would go down in history. Her family only knew that she asked a lot of questions.

When Susan was a little girl, her father, Daniel Anthony, owned a cotton mill in Adams, Massachusetts, where his employees turned cotton into thread and cloth. One day a young woman worker became sick and her doctor told her to stay home for two weeks. Susan and her sister, fourteen-year-old Guelma, wanted to take her place, but Susan's mother said no.

"Please, Mother," begged Susan.

"Absolutely not," said Mother.

"Why not?" asked Susan.

Susan was a thoughtful, observant youngster who was always questioning things that didn't make sense to her. Why did her teacher refuse to give her lessons on long division, when boys her age were learning how to do it? Why were wives and children treated like men's property? Why couldn't women have their own money or belongings? Why didn't her father seem to notice her mother's labor, which included not only raising six children but also cooking, sewing, washing, and ironing for the eleven mill workers who lived in the Anthony home? What was a mother supposed to do if her husband spent all of his wages on himself, and she wasn't allowed to get a job to support her children? Did women have to be wives and mothers? Why couldn't a woman with more experience in the mill supervise new workers who were men?

Why didn't her mother want her or Guelma to take over for the sick worker?

"It isn't proper for you to go to work," Mrs. Anthony argued. "Our family isn't poor, and you will always have a man to take care of you—your father, your brother, your husband."

But Mr. Anthony thought his daughters could learn something at the mill. Finally, Mrs. Anthony agreed to let one of the girls go. They drew straws for the opportunity. Susan won.

Susan's job was to be a "spooler"—to keep an eye on the spools, or bobbins, that held the newly spun thread. When a spool became full of thread, she had to remove it from the still-spinning machine and quickly replace it with an empty one. The work was not particularly hard or dangerous, but Susan had to be on the job six days a week, twelve hours a day.

When the two weeks were over, Mr. Anthony had a right to Susan's pay. Instead, he told her she could have it as long as she split it with Guelma, who had done Susan's household chores while Susan was working at the mill.

Susan's mother probably thought Susan's working career was over, but Susan had other ideas. Beginning at age fifteen, she took several teaching jobs. After continuing her own education, she became a girls' headmistress (principal) at a boarding school in Canajoharie, New York, when she was twenty-six. By the time she left the job, she was praised as "the smartest woman that was now or ever in Canajoharie."

Susan wanted to do more than simply earn her own living. She sought changes that would give everyone the freedom, opportunities, and privileges that only white men were granted at that time. She joined with others to end slavery. Her major life's work was on behalf of women's suffrage, that is, the right to vote in elections. Susan spent more than fifty years traveling around the country, organizing meetings, writing and giving speeches, and raising money for the cause. Because voting would give women a say in making and changing laws, Susan believed it was the most effective thing a woman could do to change her life for the better.

"It is beyond a doubt that before long women will be sent to Congress as

Representatives by some of the States," Susan said in 1900. "Indeed, it is not at all beyond the bounds of possibility that a woman may be elected President some day."

By that time, Susan's mother would have been astounded to see women working at a great many different occupations. In 1900 there were two veterinarians, 4 train engineers, 22 architects, 59 blacksmiths, 129 butchers, 208 lawyers, 219 coal miners, 337 dentists, 1,235 ministers, and 4,555 doctors who were women.

Susan never got the chance to vote. She died fourteen years before 1920, the year in which all women received that right.

Susan trained other women to carry on her work. She firmly believed that when people join with others and devote their lives to a worthy cause, "failure is impossible."

Some questions for you to think about:

- What do you think Susan B. Anthony meant when she said, "failure is impossible"? Do you agree?

- Can you imagine working for 50 years to solve a problem in the world? If so, what would it be?

- Should people who are parents also have jobs outside the home? Why, or why not?

- What are the hardest jobs you know? What makes them hard? Are they done by women, men, or both?

- Are women/girls and men/boys treated equally and fairly today? Explain.

Some things for you to do:

- Anthony's motto was "failure is impossible." Make up a motto for yourself and use it to create a bookmark, bumper sticker, T-shirt, or button.

- Imagine a meeting between Susan B. Anthony and Prudence Crandall (see "The Stone on the Mantel"). What questions would they want to ask each other and what ideas or advice would they want to share? Make up a conversation between the two of them.

- Choose at least eight important words from this story and hide them in a word search puzzle.

- Design a book jacket for a biography or autobiography of your life. Make a picture for the cover. On the inside front flap, include highlights from your life story and reasons why someone would want to read the book, and on the back tell something about the author.

- Look through the yellow pages of a large phone book. Look for ads that show people. In which jobs or services do you see women represented? Men? Both? Choose a particular line of work, such as an accountant, counselor, or pediatrician, and compare the number of men listed with the number of women.

A Good Idea

by Judy Campbell

At breakfast Raychel asked her Mom and Dad if they could have a family meeting at supper time.

"What's up?" asked her mother.

"I'm thinking of running for class president," said Raychel.

"Really? What's your platform?"

"My what?" Raychel asked.

"Platform. The things you want to see happen if you win."

"Well that's what I want to talk about at supper," said Raychel.

"O.K. I'll be home early today," her mom said. "Sounds exciting."

All day Raychel thought about running for election. She hated win-or-lose things—losing was so awful. Even when she was little, she never liked games like Farmer in the Dell, because somebody always had to be last, and she hated being last. So why in the world would she put herself in an *election*, where she could lose big time?

The answer was Colin, the other kid who was going to run for president. He was telling everybody that if he won, he would have an awesome fair in the schoolyard to raise lots of money for a huge class party. Raychel liked parties, but she thought their class should do something a little more important with the money. She wanted her class to clean up the stream that ran beside the schoolyard. It was a mess. It could be so special, but there were all kinds of junk in there. The whole school would enjoy it if it were cleaned up. Maybe the fish and turtles would even come back.

But would the other kids want to do that? She knew everyone in her Sunday school class would think it was a cool idea. They had a lot of fun doing service projects at church. But she wondered about the kids at school. Would they laugh at her idea? What if she ran and lost? She'd feel awful.

At supper she told her parents about her ideas and her feelings.

"I like your idea about the stream a lot," said Raychel's dad, "but you don't have to be class president to do it. You could just get a bunch of kids together to do it with you."

"I bet the PTO would be interested," said her mother. "They love projects like that."

"That's true," said Raychel, "but I think a class president should do something more for the school and the class than just have a party."

"I think so, too, Raychel," said her dad, "but I think you have a better chance of getting the stream cleaned up if you take your idea to the principal or to your teacher and get them to help you."

Raychel frowned. "If I go to the teacher or to another grown-up for help, then it won't be a kids' project, and I want it to be a kids' project. I want other kids to think about that polluted, clogged-up stream, and I want kids to clean it up. Our class could do something important for the school and for the fish and the turtles and the whole town."

She took a deep breath and announced, "I've made up my mind. I'm going to do it. I'm going to run for class president."

Raychel's parents looked at each other and smiled. They knew that when Raychel made up her mind about something, nothing would stop her.

"Okay, honey," said her dad. "Where do we start?"

"Thanks, Dad, but I really do want this to be a kids' project. I'll start tomorrow morning by telling the teacher and the other students."

"Well, good luck. You know where you can come for help if you need it."

For the next two weeks, Raychel and her campaign team made posters, talked to other kids, and made plans to clean up the stream if Raychel was elected.

As election day drew closer, Raychel and her team began to worry. Colin had a lot of kids on his side. He even talked about getting one of those big, air-filled jumping castles they have a real carnivals. What kids would choose to stand knee-deep in cold, dirty water, picking up slimy trash, instead of jumping around inside a blown-up castle?

"Mom, Dad, I need to talk," Raychel said at supper one night. "A lot of kids want to clean up the stream, and they'll vote for me." Raychel paused. "But I'm pretty sure that more kids want to have a huge party. I'm afraid I'm going to lose," she said, fighting back tears.

"Well, you have two more days to wait," said her dad. "Let's think about what you'll do if Colin does win."

"I'll feel stupid, that's what I'll do," wailed Raychel. "All the kids will laugh at me. I'll be 'Raychel the loser'!"

"No," said her mom, "you'll be Raychel the person with a really good idea who didn't get elected class president because most of the kids would rather party than work. Lots of people with great ideas don't get elected president. But you know, good ideas are good ideas, and people will work to make them happen. What is more important to you, cleaning up the stream or being class president?"

Raychel thought a minute. In the beginning, cleaning up the stream was all she thought about. Now that she'd been campaigning, though, she'd begun to think it would be fun to be president. And winning would be a lot more fun than losing.

"I guess I don't really know," she answered.

"I know how much you want to win," said her dad, "but I also know how much this stream means to you. I bet you won't give up on it, no matter what happens in the election."

On election day Raychel went to school trying to look her best, but she was afraid. Lots of kids came up to her and told her they wanted the stream cleaned up. Some kids admitted that they wanted a party, too. Raychel knew lots of kids were having a hard time deciding.

The election was held after lunch. Even before the votes were counted, Raychel knew she hadn't won. Most of the kids looked right past her after they voted, instead of looking at her, the way her friends did.

When the announcement was made, she felt like running away. Instead, she stood up and thanked the kids who had worked with her, and the teachers who helped, and she shook Colin's hand and congratulated him.

She had practiced in her mind how to be a good loser. But she was not ready for what the new president did next. Colin stood up, and he, too, thanked everyone for their help and for their votes. He came over to shake Raychel's hand.

After that, he turned to the class and said, "Raychel had a great idea about cleaning up the stream, and I think there is a way to do both things—to have a party and clean up the stream. We could have a work party first and then a fun party. What do you think, Raychel?"

"Sure," Raychel said, beaming. And then she remembered: A good idea is a good idea, no matter who wins or loses.

Some questions for you to think about:

- Do you think you would have voted for Raychel or Colin? Why?

- What does it mean to "feel like a loser"? What is a "good loser"?

- What makes a good candidate? What kind of information is helpful when people are deciding whom to vote for?

- In what ways can kids have a voice and a vote about things that concern them?

- If you were running in some kind of election, what would your platform be?

Some things for you to do:

- Imagine you are running for some kind of office. Make a campaign poster for yourself.

- Pretend you get elected to that office. Write an imaginary newspaper article about your greatest accomplishment, or draw a picture to look like a photograph of it, and write a caption to go underneath.

- What problem would you like to see solved in your school or community? Write a letter to your student council, school principal, or the editor of your newspaper, sharing your ideas.

- Identify a natural area near you that is being polluted by trash, and recruit a group of people to help you clean it up. (Ask an adult to help you develop safety rules.)

- Plan the coolest party you can imagine for a particular group of people, such as your family, class, sports team, or scout troop. Let your imagination run wild. Decide when and where you would hold the party, what you would eat and drink, and what you would do. Design creative invitations.

We Should
Care for
Our Earth
and Its Plants
and Animals

Reverence for Life

by Ruth Gibson

Albert Schweitzer was a famous minister and doctor who helped poor and sick people in Africa in the early decades of the 1900s. His desire to help all living things had always been a part of him, even when he was a child. In fact, one day after school, young Albert raced home long before dinner time. Almost in tears, he burst in the door.

"What happened?" asked his mom, kneeling down to examine him.

"A fight."

"A fight? Are you hurt?"

"It wasn't exactly that kind of fight," said Albert.

It's true that there had been a fight. All the boys in the neighborhood had called him names and thrown rocks at him. But that wasn't why Albert was so upset. The real trouble was the birds. Albert and the others had been shooting at the nesting birds with their slingshots and smashing the nests with sticks.

"I did it, too, Mama," said Albert. "But then I saw what I had done, and I felt so awful. It is a terrible thing, what we were doing. If you can discover where the birds make their nests, if you can come up so close you can see the mother bird, sitting on her eggs, with her eyes so bright, and not frighten her away, well, that is something wonderful! And I'm the one who showed the other boys where the nests are."

"Why?" Mother asked.

"I wanted them to admire me because I knew something they didn't know," Albert explained. "And I showed them how to come close, slowly and quietly. Then one of them tried to scare the mother bird away. But she wouldn't fly. She wouldn't leave her nest. I always thought I was so clever to find the birds on their nest before they flew off. I thought they didn't see me. But now I know. The mother sees everything. It's because she's brave that she doesn't leave her nest, not because I'm clever."

Albert and his mom sat down.

"They tried to scare her away," Albert continued, "and we all hit the tree and the branches with sticks. And the other birds flew over our heads, shrieking. When some of the boys took out their slingshots, I tried to stop them, but they wouldn't listen. I screamed at them. I tried to push them, and when they killed the mother bird, I got so mad, I hit a boy with my stick. Then everyone laughed at me, and that's when they threw stones at me. So I ran away, but they kept hitting the tree, and they knocked down the nest and smashed it."

110

Albert's mother knew there was no point in scolding Albert. He had learned a valuable lesson, the hard way.

Albert often chose to play alone after that. The other boys teased him for a while, but soon they tired of it. Besides nature, Albert loved music. He began taking organ lessons and learned quickly; as a teenager, he was asked to play the organ in church when the regular organist was ill. In college Albert studied to become a minister. He also continued with his organ lessons.

Why do people choose the paths they do? We know Albert remembered these experiences from his childhood because he talked about them as an adult. Perhaps they encouraged him to choose work that would persuade others to do things that are good instead of destructive. Though well liked and respected as a minister, Albert felt nervous while preaching sermons and going to hospitals, trying to comfort the sick and the dying. He began questioning whether he had chosen the right path. He had heard that in many parts of Africa, people suffered from diseases that could be cured with newly discovered medicines and techniques, but there weren't many doctors interested in working in Africa. Most doctors wanted to stay in their own countries, where they could speak their own language and work in familiar surroundings.

At the age of 30, Albert became a medical student. After his graduation, he and his wife went to Africa, a place where there were no other doctors to work with him, where Albert was to build a hospital near the village of Lambarene.

The people of Lambarene were suspicious at first. "You know what these white people are like," they said to each other. "They do not follow the traditions of our people.

They will do strange things. They will try to force us to do what they wish, they will take what they want, and they will make trouble for us. They always do."

But Albert surprised everybody. Instead of trying to put up a building that looked like the European hospitals he had worked in, he asked the people of Lambarene to show him their houses and to teach him their way of building. Built in this Lambarene way, his hospital looked strange to the Europeans who visited him—but not to the African people.

When people were sick, Albert did not tell them to ignore the teachings of the village healers. Instead, he worked with the Lambarene elders to learn about their healing traditions. In return, Albert showed them the things he knew. Albert also ignored European rules restricting visitors. In his hospital, the families of sick people were allowed to camp in the hospital yard. They helped care for their ill family members and prepared their food. Albert discovered that it takes more than medicine, surgery, and science to heal the sick. When people can have loved ones near them, and eat their favorite foods, they often get well sooner.

Albert figured out a way to protect his organ from the humid jungle climate. After a long day at work, playing the organ was a special joy for him.

Albert's childhood love for animals remained with him till the day he died, in Lambarene, at the age of ninety. No one was allowed to kill animals around his hospital, unless they were needed for food. His pet cats ran freely through the hospital. One day, when he was watching the hippopotami that came to the river to drink, a new idea came to him. In that moment, he understood very clearly the influence that was most important to him: reverence for life—to protect and care for all living things. And that was the light that guided his life.

Some questions for you to think about:

- Has peer pressure ever led you to do something you regretted? If so, what happened?

- How would you describe "reverence for life"? What does it mean to live with a sense of reverence for life?

- What do you imagine Albert's wife was like?

- What do you like to do now that you think you will still like to do by the time you are an adult?

- What do you think you want to do with your life when you become an adult? Why?

Some things for you to do:

- Pretend you are creating a coloring book about Albert Schweitzer's life, for early elementary school children. Make a simple outline drawing illustrating a part of this story, and at the bottom write a sentence or two that describes what is happening in the picture.

■ Design a hospital that is just for children. Draw a floor plan, showing the special things you would include to encourage child patients to feel more at home and to help them get well.

■ Illustrate the words "reverence for life." Make the letters look like plants or animals, or put pictures of living things inside the letters. (Draw them or cut them out from magazines.)

■ Interview an adult who has a job that interests you. Ask: Did you imagine having this kind of job when you were growing up? Have you had other jobs before this one? What do you like best about your job? What do you like least? What advice would you give others who want to get into this line of work?

■ Go outside and spend at least five minutes observing a living thing (plant or animal), using as many of your senses as possible, or pick one of your favorite plants or animals and write a poem about it or draw a picture of it.

Bird Mother

by Erin Dajka

Summer vacation had just begun, and I had gone with my friend Anthea to the barn where she kept her horse, Bucky. We began to exercise him in the indoor arena and noticed that he seemed to be staying away from one particular spot. When we went to investigate the spot, we discovered some baby birds lying in the sand. Four had fallen close to thirty feet from their nest, but only two had survived. I did not know if they had died from the impact of the fall or from lack of food and water.

Anthea figured her family wouldn't let her take the birds home, but I knew I could not leave the two survivors to the fate of their siblings. I found an old Kleenex box and laid some tissues in it to make a kind of nest for them.

The birds were almost newborns. They had only a tiny bit of fluff on their spines and wings, their eyes were not open, and their beaks were still pliable. They were not even chirping. My parents and I assumed that the birds would not survive the night, but we did not want them to pass uncomfortably. So, I force fed them warm milk from an eyedropper, replaced the Kleenex box with a little bucket, and wrapped the birds up in a tissue to keep them warm.

When I woke the next morning, I was amazed to hear noises coming from my closet, where I had left the birds to sleep. Though they had been completely silent the night before, they now were making very quiet chirping sounds. I couldn't believe they were still alive! My heart melted; they were so small and fragile, and they looked naked because they hadn't grown any feathers yet.

The birds had their heads back and their beaks wide open. My mother had gotten in touch with a bird expert, who told us to feed the birds puppy chow. The expert also advised us that they were most likely robins, since their beaks were yellow and fairly hard.

I borrowed a cage from a friend of mine who kept parrots and other large tropical birds. It was entirely too big for my little babies; their feet slipped through the bars in the bottom. But when the birds got older, and grew feathers, they had enough room to flap around a bit. I always kept the cage out of sight of our cats.

At first I loved my little birds. I felt like a mother to two adorable creatures, and I enjoyed watching them grow. From day to day, there were big changes in their size and feathers. When the feathers first appeared, they looked nothing like feathers. They were spiny-looking, blackish grey, and they came out only on the tails and wings. Later, they began to grow in all over. The spines got longer and longer until they finally opened up and began to look like feathers.

The bird expert told us that once the tail feathers were about an inch and a half long, the birds would start to try flying. I didn't have to teach them anything—they just started flapping around in their cage. Eventually, I let them free in my bedroom (with the door closed and the kitties elsewhere). However, each time I let them out, it was a serious pain trying to catch them again and put them back in their cage.

As the birds grew in size, they also grew more annoying. Their chirping was very loud—especially early in the morning. They also became harder to take care of. They needed me to clean out their cage and to be there every hour to soften their food and feed them, but I was already busy with other things most of the time.

When I brought the birds home, I thought that they would be cute and fun. Somehow, I had the idea that I could take care of them when I wanted to and that they would wait around until I wanted to have fun with them. But that wasn't the way it worked. Instead, I always had to be there for them. I had to work my life around what they needed, and that frustrated me.

The bird expert told me that it would probably take two months before the little robins would be grown up enough to do well on their own. I tried to push them along to make them grow up faster so that I could relieve myself of the burden of taking care of them. I felt bad about that—and still do—but I didn't want to spend two months taking care of them.

Finally, after over a month of being constantly annoyed by the responsibility of their care, I was ready to let them go. I have no idea whether or not they were ready to leave, but perhaps they were just as ready to get rid of their human caretaker as I was to get rid of them. I took their cage outside and removed the top. The birds just sat there for the longest time. Finally, I went inside and left them. When I came back, they were gone.

I left the cage outside for a few days, just in case they needed to return, but I never saw them again. Honestly, I was relieved, though I worried about their chances for survival. One of the birds had a weak leg and could never use it very well, and I have no way of knowing if the birds could find enough food or if they kept out of the way of the crows.

To this day, I wonder if I made the right decisions. The question of whether or not I was a good "mother" to "my" birds nags at me.

Some questions for you to think about:

- What kinds of experiences have you had with animals in or from the wild?
- Did Erin do the right thing in rescuing the birds? Why or why not?
- What personality traits might make someone good at caring for young or injured animals?
- How did you feel at the end of the story? Why?
- What do you think Erin learned from this experience?

Some things for you to do:

■ Rewrite this story from the perspective of one of the birds.

■ Review Erin's description of what the baby birds looked like and then make a picture of them, using paint or colored chalk, or make a sculpture out of clay.

■ Make a diorama of a scene from this story.

■ Talk to someone who is an expert in rescuing wild creatures. (Check with veterinarians and nature centers.)

■ Make a list of all the species of domestic birds that you can name. Obtain a bird guide and find out how many different species live in your area. See how many species you observe during a walk in your neighborhood or nearby park or nature preserve.

Other Stories You Might Like

If you liked the stories offered in this book, try these other books with similar themes.

If Christmas Eve Happened Today

Love Song for a Baby, by Marion Dane Bauer. Simon & Schuster Books for Young Readers, 2002.

On the Day You Were Born, by Debra Frasier. Harcourt, 1995.

Welcoming Babies, by Margy Burns Knight. Tilbury House Publishers, 1998.

When You Were a Baby, by Deborah Shaw Lewis. Peachtree Publishers, 1995.

The Night You Were Born, by Wendy McCormick. Peachtree Publishers, 2000.

Give the Ball to Peetie

Cleversticks, by Bernard Ashley. Random House, 1995.

He's My Brother, by Joe Lasker. Albert Whitman & Co., 1987.

Different Just Like Me, by Lori Mitchell. Charlesbridge, 1999.

Extraordinary Friends, by Fred Rogers. Puffin, 2000.

We'll Paint the Octopus Red, by Stephanie Stuve-Bodeen. Woodbine House, 1998.

The Stone on the Mantel

A Bus of Our Own, by Freddi Evans. Albert Whitman & Co., 2001.

Dear Willie Rudd, by Libba Moore Gray. Aladdin Paperbacks, 2000.

Freedom School, Yes!, by Amy Littlesugar. Philomel Books, 2001.

Going Someplace Special, by Patricia C. McKissak. Atheneum, 2001.

Uncle Jed's Barbershop, by Margaree King Mitchell. Aladdin Paperbacks, 1998.

Brown Shoes

Whoever You Are, by Mem Fox. Harcourt, 1997.

Amazing Grace, by Mary Hoffman. Scott Foresman, 1991.

All the Colors We Are, by Katie Kissinger. Redleaf Press, 1997.

This Is Our House, by Michael Rosen. Candlewick Press, 1998.

Black Like Kyra, White Like Me, by Judith Vigna. Albert Whitman & Co., 1996.

Mistakes

Big Al, by Andrew Clements. Aladdin Paperbacks, 1997.

Today Was a Terrible Day, by Patricia Reilly Giff. Viking Press, 1984.

Ooops!, by Suzy Kline. Puffin Books, 1989.

Nobody's Perfect . . . Not Even My Mother, by Norma Simon. Albert Whitman & Co., 1987.

The Teacher from the Black Lagoon, by Mike Tholer. Scholastic Trade, 1989.

The Day the Turkey Walked

Turkey Pox, by Laurie Anderson. Albert Whitman & Co., 1998.

Circle of Thanks, by Susi Fowler. Scholastic Trade, 2001.

Thanksgiving Wish, by Michael Rosen. Blue Sky Press, 1999.

Thanksgiving at the Tappletons, by Eileen Spinelli. Scott Foresman, 1992.

Giving Thanks, by Chief Jake Swamp. Lee & Low Books, 1997.

A Candle for Us

Adoption Stories for Young Children, by Randall B. Hicks. Wordslinger Press, 1994.

Beginnings, by Virginia L. Kroll. Concept Books, 1994.

Who's in a Family?, by Robert Skutch. Tricycle Press, 1998.

Grandmother's Gift

The Mountains of Tibet, by Mordicai Gerstein. HarperTrophy, 1989.

Lifetimes, by Bryan Mellonie. Bantam Doubleday Dell Publishers, 1987.

What on Earth Do You Do When Someone Dies?, by Trevor Romain. Free Spirit, 1999.

Badger's Parting Gifts, by Susan Varley. Mulberry Books, 1992.

The Great Change, by White Deer of Autumn. Beyond Words Publishing Co., 1992.

A Little Jar Labeled Freedom

Terrible Things, by Eve Bunting. Jewish Publication Society, 1996. (This story may be too scary for younger children.)

Beginnings of Earth and Sky, by Sophia Lyon Fahs and Dorothy T. Spoerl. Beacon Press, 1974.

The Fire Children, by Eric Madden. Dial Books for Young Readers, 1993.

Light, by Sarah Waldman. Harcourt, 1993.

The Two-Legged Creature, by Anna Lee Walters. Northland Publishers, 1993.

Answer Mountain

What Makes Me Happy?, by Catherine and Laurence Anholt. Pearson Learning, 1998.

What Is Love?, by Etan Boritzer. Veronica Lane Books, 1997.

The Wise Woman and Her Secret, by Eve Merriam. Aladdin Paperbacks, 1999.

Why Does That Man Have Such a Big Nose?, by Mary Beth Quinsey. Parenting Press, 1986.

Who Is Ben?, by Charlotte Zolotow. HarperCollins, 1997.

Grady Asks Why

Gregory's Shadow, by Don Freeman. Puffin, 2002.

Possum and the Peeper, by Anne Hunter. Sandpiper, 2000.

Gretchen Groundhog, It's Your Day, by Abby Levine. Albert Whitman & Co., 2002.

16 Miles to Spring, by Andrew Pelletier. Albert Whitman & Co., 2002.

Mud, by Mary Lyn Ray. Voyager Books, 2001.

Rainbow Crow, by Nancy Van Laan. Econo-Clad Books, 1999.

Paperwhite, by Nancy Elizabeth Wallace. Houghton Mifflin Co., 2000.

The Children's Crusade

White Socks Only, by Evelyn Coleman. Albert Whitman & Co., 1999.

The Story of Ruby Bridges, by Robert Coles. Scholastic Trade, 2000.

All the Colors of the Earth, by Sheila Hamanaka. Mulberry Books, 1999.

Happy Birthday, Martin Luther King, by Jean Marzollo. Scholastic Trade, 1995.

The People Who Hugged Trees, by Deborah Lee Rose. Robert Rinehart Publishers, 2001.

The Evil Wizard

Beware the Dragon, by Sarah Wilson. Harper and Row, 1985.

"The Half-Boy," in *Old Tales for a New Day,* by Sophia Lyon Fahs and Alice Cobb. Prometheus Books, 1992.

Miss Fanshawe and the Great Dragon Adventure, by Sue Scuillard. St. Martin's Press, 1987.

Spite Fences

Paul and Sebastian, by Rene Escudie. Kane/Miller Book Publishers, 1994.

Old Henry, by Joan W. Blos. Mulberry Books, 1990.

Chester's Way, by Kevin Henkes. Mulberry Books, 1997.

The Ugly Vegetables, by Grace Lin. Talewinds, 1999.

Making Friends, by Margaret Mahy. Macmillan, 1990.

What If Nobody Forgave?

Even If I Did Something Awful, by Barbara Shook Hazen. Aladdin Paperbacks, 1992.

Bajo la Luna de Limón, by Edith Hope. Fine, Lee and Low Books, 1999.

Dinah's Mad, Bad Wishes, by Barbara Joose. HarperCollins Children's Books, 1989.

Giant John, by Arnold Lobel. HarperCollins Publishers, 1987.

Susan Goes to Work

Extraordinary Girls, by Maya Ajmera. Charlesbridge Publishing, 2000.

Piggybook, by Anthony Browne. Knopf, 1990.

I'm a Girl, by Lili Jukes. Cool Kids Press, 1995.

She Is Born, by Virginia Kroll. Beyond Words Publishing Co., 2000.

Girl, You're Amazing, by Virginia Kroll. Albert Whitman and Company, 2001.

Nobody Owns the Sky, by Reeve Lindbergh. Candlewick Press, 1998.

All by Herself: 14 Girls Who Made a Difference, by Ann Whitford Paul. Raintree/Steck Vaughn, 2000.

Elizabeth Cady Stanton, by Carol Hilgartner Schlank et al. Gryphon House, 1993.

A Good Idea

Rachel Carson, by William Accorsi. Holiday House, 1993.

The Wartville Wizard, by Don Madden. Aladdin Paperbacks, 1993.

Earth Book for Kids, by Linda Schwartz. Learning Works, 1990.

Dear World: How Children Around the World Feel About Our Environment, edited by Lanis Temple. Random House, 1993.

Courage, by Bernard Waber. Houghton Mifflin Company, 2002.

Reverence for Life

Our Big Home, by Linda Glaser. Millbrook Press, 2000.

Each Living Thing, by Joanne Ryder. Gulliver Books, 2000.

In Our Image, by Nancy Sohn Swartz. Jewish Lights Publishers, 1998.

Village Tree, by Taro Yashima. Viking Press, 1972.

Making the World, by Douglas Wood. Simon & Schuster, 1998.

Bird Mother

The Bat in the Boot, by Annie Cannon. Orchard Books, 1996.

Animal Rescue, by Susan E. Goodman. Aladdin Paperbacks, 2001.

Nora's Duck, by Satomi Ichikawa. Philomel Books, 1991.

Washing the Willow Tree Loon, by Jacqueline Briggs Martin. Simon & Schuster Books, 1995.

Sterling, by Sandra Verrill White and Michael Filisky. Crown Publishers, 1989.

About the Contributors

The Reverend Paul Beckel was born in Wadena, Minnesota, in 1964. He currently serves as a minister in Wausau, Wisconsin, and lives with his wife, Jane Robins Beckel. They have three children: Rick, Ben, and Jonathan.

The Reverend Shannon Bernard was a Unitarian Universalist minister and a story-teller at heart. "If Christmas Happened Today" was inspired by her desire for the children of her church to have access to the basic message of Jesus' birth and for adults and children alike to claim the potential in their own lives. It has grown and changed each year in the retelling. Shannon died of cancer before this book went to press but was delighted at the opportunity to leave this story behind for all of us.

The Reverend Judy Campbell serves a congregation on Martha's Vineyard. Prior to ordination she was a professor of art at Lesley University in Cambridge, Massachusetts. She is the author of two books on watercolor painting, a book of poetry, and a children's book, and she is currently a staff writer for *uu & me!* magazine.

Erin Margit Dajka is currently studying at Grinnell College in Iowa, majoring in religious studies. Her story is a revised version of a true story she wrote as an essay for college applications.

The Reverend Ruth Gibson insisted in childhood that her unchurched parents find her a Sunday school. Now she is a minister of religious education and gets to go to Sunday school, where she enjoys sharing and hearing stories—as much as she likes. Ruth has served congregations in Worcester and Boston, Massachusetts; Madison, Wisconsin; and Denver, Colorado.

The Reverend Cynthia B. Johnson was an elementary school teacher, day care director, writer for the development office in a university, teacher of bridge, and most abidingly, a community volunteer specializing in education and government before entering the ministry, in midlife. Before retiring with her husband to Door County, Wisconsin, she served a congregation in Oklahoma City. Cynthia, who is also a poet, wrote this creation story to accompany a sermon on evil.

The Reverend Barbara Marshman ministered to children for sixty of her eighty-six years of life. They adored her, and she in turn loved and respected them. Along with Charlene Brotman and the Reverend Ann Fields, she wrote *Why Do Bad Things Happen?*, *How Can I Know What to Believe?*, *Holidays and Holy Days*, and *The UU Kids Book*.

The Reverend Colleen M. McDonald has loved to write since she was a child, and she has enjoyed telling stories since she became a minister, in 1988; three of her stories in this anthology were based on her own experiences. She lives with her husband, two daughters, and three cats in Rockford, Illinois, where she participates in a monthly writing group.

The Reverend Kate Rohde is a Unitarian Universalist minister serving the Unitarian Fellowship of West Chester, Pennsylvania. She has always loved good stories.

Dr. Joshua Searle-White is a clinical psychologist who has been writing and telling stories of adventure and imagination for ten years. His stories are lighthearted and humorous and invite the listener to open up to new experiences. He lives with his wife and two daughters in Meadville, Pennsylvania, where he teaches in the psychology department at Allegheny College.

Sarah Skwire lives with her husband and two cats in Indianapolis, Indiana, where she is a fellow at Liberty Fund, Inc. She wrote "Answer Mountain" for her mother, who is a minister, to tell to her congregation. Sarah's poems have appeared, among other places, in *Oxford Magazine* and *The Vocabula Review* and are forthcoming in the *New Criterion*.

The Reverend Gary Smith has been senior minister of the First Parish in Concord, Massachusetts, since 1988. He has worked for the Unitarian Universalist Association at its headquarters in Boston and has served churches in Middletown, Connecticut, and Bangor, Maine. It was in Maine where the story of Peetie and the wonderful basketball game actually took place, around 1980. The oral story arose out of an interfaith minister's storytelling group. David Glusker, a Methodist minister, fashioned the story into words, and Gary wrote it down for his appearance before the Unitarian Universalist Ministerial Fellowship Committee.